Elizabet.

Biography

The Jewel in the Hollywood Crown

By Isabelle Valdez

TABLE OF CONTENTS

ELIZABETH TAYLOR

The Jewel in Hollywood's Crown
BIOGRAPHY

CHAPTER 1
A New Star Is Born

Elizabeth Rosemond Taylor was born in London on February 27, 1932, to American parents Sara (Sothern), an actress, and Francis, an art dealer. Sara's mother, Elizabeth Ann Wilson, was born in 1864, and Elizabeth was named for her. Sara had a flair for the dramatic, which she passed on to her daughter, and she claimed to be related to Mary Stuart, Queen of Scots. Sara and Francis had a son called Howard two years before, and Sara had been praying for a girl this time. She was a devoted Christian Scientist who thought that God was always present to hear her prayers. Sara's mother had urged her while she was pregnant with their boy to fill her head with "beautiful thoughts" in order to have a beautiful kid. She reasoned that it had to have worked. Sara said that when Howard was born, he resembled a "Botticelli angel," with blond locks and beautiful blue eyes. Her hopes were partially realized on that frigid February morning in London in 1932. Sara almost recoiled in horror when the infant Elizabeth Taylor was given to her mother, wrapped in a cashmere shawl. "Her hair was dark and lengthy. Her ears were coated in thick black fuzz and inlaid into the sides of her skull; her nose was a tip-tilted button, and her little face was so tightly clenched it appeared as if it would never open." What good were all those "beautiful thoughts"? She worried whether she hadn't given her second child enough care in the womb and was now being punished as a result.

Sara, who was a little too superficial, hoped that her daughter's appearance would improve, and it did, in the most astonishing way. Elizabeth went from not talking until she was more than a year old—unlike Howard, who began talking when he was six months old—to talking and gurgling at the same time. "Her hair had long since vanished from her arms, back, and ears; now, nature seemed determined to make her beautiful!" "Her eyes grew larger," Sara wrote in a 1954 Ladies' Home Journal piece called "Elizabeth, My Daughter." "Double rows of long, black eyelashes made shadowy frames for those deep pools of blue." Elizabeth's change was complete by the time she was a year and a half old. Sara made certain that her own transformation from caterpillar to butterfly was weaved throughout the story of her daughter's existence.

Elizabeth's parents were childhood acquaintances who met in Kansas City. When Francis relocated to New York to work for his Uncle Howard Young, a multimillionaire art dealer with a well-known New York gallery, and Sara began an acting career, they lost touch. She altered her surname from Warmbrodt to Sothern and dropped the h in "Sarah" after searching the phone book with her mother for suitable stage names. She and Francis met at the glitzy Mayfair Ball, hosted at the Ritz-Carlton in New York in 1927. Sara, who wore her hair in a trendy bob and had large black eyes, determined that evening that she had found the man she was going to marry. They got married after two weeks. Sara was the one who proposed it. When she asked Francis, who was timid in comparison, why he hadn't proposed yet, he answered she was "too big a star."

The Taylors married and lived comfortably because of the generosity of two donors, Uncle Howard and conservative British MP Victor Cazalet. Sara had cleverly befriended Cazalet's sister while she was playing in a London play. Cazalet even provided them with a weekend getaway home. Francis suspected an affair because Sara was intoxicated by Cazalet's wealth and influence. The Taylors relocated to London because Francis's uncle asked his nephew to oversee his London gallery. They lived in Hampstead, a London suburb. Their home on Wildwood Road overlooked Hampstead Heath and included a lovely garden with three-foot-high yellow tulips, lavender violas, a formal rose garden that terraced down to the heath, and a tennis court. Heathwood was the name given to the house.

Cazalet was dubbed Elizabeth's godfather, and he helped them maintain their upper-class lifestyle, which included a driver, two maids, and a nanny. Elizabeth spent her summers and weekends with her family in Little Swallows, a beautiful sixteenth-century brick guest cottage covered with green moss. The mansion was on Cazalet's Great Swifts estate in Cranbrook, Kent, about sixty miles from London. Cazalet gave Elizabeth a New Forest pony named Betty when she was three years old. Elizabeth remarked decades later that it was the finest period of her life since it was the one time she was permitted to be a child. She enjoyed riding across lush meadows because "the isolation, solitude, companionship with an animal... it's a marvelous therapeutic kind of thing." That's when Sara realized Elizabeth had a special bond with animals. Betty once threw Elizabeth and Howard off her back and into a stinging nettle patch. "She flattened her body out on Betty's bareback, put her arms around her neck, and kept talking to her as she rode off over the fields, while we stood there with our mouths hanging open," Sara remembered. They became pals that day. This style of 'gentling' horses (or any animal) led to her portraying the character of Velvet," Elizabeth's breakout role as Velvet Brown in National Velvet. Elizabeth adored her older brother, and their friendship lasted the rest of her life. They both liked attributes in each other: Elizabeth admired Howard's free spirit, and Howard admired Elizabeth's tenacity. She enjoyed watching her elder brother box and shouted with delight whenever he landed a left punch on his opponent's jaw. She even persuaded her parents to buy her boxing gloves, and she requested that Howard practice on her before a bout. She relished the part of the feisty little sister.

Sara realized the effect Elizabeth's beauty had on people, and she made sure that her daughter was given every opportunity to mingle with the elite. She enrolled her in dance lessons at the prestigious Vacani School of Dance, where two generations of British royalty had gone. When Elizabeth was three and a half years old, she performed in a benefit recital held in Queen's Hall. In the audience was the other most famous Elizabeth of her era, the young Princess Elizabeth and her sister Princess Margaret. Sara was in heaven. Elizabeth could fulfill her abandoned dream—she could become the star that Sara had always wanted to be. "The house went wild!" she wrote, remembering the curtain going up and down several times as Elizabeth sat there in the center of the stage. Then life changed suddenly and forever on the cusp of World War II. Elizabeth's childhood gathering primroses and bluebells and riding horses in the rolling green hills of the English countryside was over. If the war had not happened, Elizabeth later said, she probably would have become an English debutante and stayed married to one man with a solid job and had lots of children. But fate decided otherwise. After having tea with Winston Churchill, who was not yet prime minister but who was a hugely influential politician, Cazalet took Francis aside and told him that he should send Sara, Elizabeth, and Howard to the United States immediately. Elizabeth's last time at Little Swallows was Easter 1939. Like thousands of other Americans who fled England, the Taylors were literally running for their lives.

Once they relocated to Los Angeles, Sara became singularly obsessed with making her daughter a star. Their opulent lifestyle belied their dwindling bank account. They were down to their last twenty-five dollars, and Francis, who was still in England, could not send them money because of the war. They cut down on living expenses, the biggest sacrifice being living without red meat, which was nothing compared to the deprivation some people faced during the war. It had been a narrow escape; just five months later England declared war on Germany. They lost their English accents and Sara became "Mother" instead of "Mummy." But Elizabeth was desperately homesick. She sat in her room listening to classical music and wept when she thought about England and the countryside she had loved.

Sara wished to channel Elizabeth's energy into her professional endeavors. Every night, she read to her from her Christian Science Bible. Elizabeth highlighted one passage in particular: "Love inspires, illuminates, designates, and leads the way." Right intentions offer thought opinions, as well as strength and freedom of voice and action." If this mother-daughter duo wanted something badly enough, they would get it. Sara's reason for living had become Elizabeth. Every room in their new California home featured six to twelve photos of her daughter. Francis must have been surprised when he rejoined them in Los Angeles. While Francis and Howard ate in solitude, Sara spoke with Elizabeth about acting and film projects. (After Sara died in 1994, Elizabeth's lawyer, Barbara Berkowitz, went to Sara's home in Palm Desert, California, to assist in gathering her items.

Francis was becoming increasingly concerned about Sara's undivided concentration on Elizabeth. She had Elizabeth repeat her role in The Fool for practice. She showed Elizabeth how to cry on command. Francis stood helpless while Sara lectured Elizabeth on proper manners, striking a target, and finding her key light. The truth was that she had never achieved the professional success she desired, and marriage and children had failed to fill the emptiness. Sara stated that she tried to avoid having Elizabeth audition for movie roles, but it is evident that she was determined to make her daughter a great celebrity. Sara and Francis rented a home in Pacific Palisades, where Elizabeth attended the same school as the children of famous studio head and movie producer Darryl Zanuck and actress Norma Shearer. Weekends at the Zanucks' pool and afternoons with Shearer's family were more than just playdates; they were intended to introduce Elizabeth to Hollywood's powerful people. Sara took matters into her own hands when she did not instantly get her film roles.
Sara claims she was out shopping with Elizabeth one Saturday morning when she came across Francis' new art gallery at the

Beverly Hills Hotel's arcade level on Sunset Boulevard. The gallery displayed artworks that Francis had brought from England before the war began. They dropped by to "see Dad" and ended up having lunch with Reggie Allen, the head of the story department at Universal Studios, and Andrea Berens, who was about to marry J. Cheever Cowdin, Universal's chairman. Berens was to Francis' gallery because she had her portrait made by Augustus John, a prominent Welsh portrait artist, and knew Francis carried his work. Sara made sure Elizabeth and Berens had time to converse while the deal was being finalized. Before Berens went, she stated, "Cheever must see this child." Sara was more than pleased to oblige, and she invited Cowdin and Berens to tea the following Sunday. It was now up to Elizabeth to make a good first impression on Cowdin. Sara and Elizabeth sat with her Christian Science prayer book the afternoon before her test at Universal, and Sara instructed her to imagine only pleasant things. After all, that kind of thinking had converted her daughter into a beauty, and Sara believed it might turn her into a celebrity. Sara took Elizabeth to a music class consisting of other children with well-connected parents soon after she tested at Universal.

According to Sara, "Elizabeth's voice rose like a bird; she sang with all the joy of her heart." When she finished, the room exploded in applause. Carmen wanted Elizabeth to meet her husband, who was working at MGM at the time. When Sara informed Carmen about the Universal audition, Carmen promised not to sign Elizabeth with Universal until she could audition for MGM. Shrewdly planned to play MGM off of Universal and informed Cowdin of MGM's offer. He doubled the money to the then-hefty figure of $200 per week, and Elizabeth agreed to a seven-year contract with Universal. Sara expected Elizabeth to get more attention because Universal was a smaller studio. Elizabeth, on the other hand, favored MGM, where Katharine Hepburn, Lana Turner, and Clark Gable backed up the studio's famed slogan that it had "more stars than there are in the heavens." Mayer, on the other hand, boosted, promoted, and sometimes destroyed such stars.

Nonetheless, signing with Universal proved to be a disastrous mistake. Elizabeth made her film debut in 1942, at the age of eleven, in There's One Born Every Minute, alongside Carl Switzer, who portrayed Alfalfa in Our Gang. The film was a flop, and her role was not challenging. Universal did not renew her option a year later, and she was out of employment. After Universal dropped her in the summer of 1942, Sara invited Elizabeth to visit Hopper in the hopes that Hopper would write something favorable about Elizabeth or introduce her to another studio boss. Elizabeth performed her favorite song, "Blue Danube," but Hopper was underwhelmed. Hopper stated that Elizabeth's future did not "lie in her singing." Hopper didn't have anything further to say. Elizabeth's earnings had been extremely beneficial to the family during the war, and they had utilized them to fund their luxurious lifestyle. By then, the Taylors had relocated from Pacific Palisades to a huge Mediterranean-style mansion on Elm Drive in Beverly Hills, complete with a red-tiled roof. Sara had to find another way back into MGM. She discovered it through Francis, an air-raid warden in charge of guarding the area in case the war came to America. He became friends with Sam Marx, another neighborhood warden. Marx happened to be an MGM producer working on a film called Lassie Come Home. They needed a young girl with a British accent, but they couldn't find one because World War II was raging in Europe. Because the British partners in the struggle against fascism, there was a lot of pro-British attitude in the United States.

Francis nominated his daughter, and Marx told him she needed to come straight away if she wanted to be considered for the position. That afternoon, twenty-five girls had already auditioned, and the audition ended at 6:00 p.m. Sara and Elizabeth came at 5:45, and they were on the verge of choosing one of the auditioned females because no one expected much from Elizabeth. Sara will not let her daughter miss out on this opportunity since she had seen how quickly a dream might go. Elizabeth could only read the script once. Despite Sara's pressure, Elizabeth thoroughly enjoyed the encounter. "It was like magic," she described it, "living out every young girl's fantasy." MGM offered her a long-term deal for $75 per week, which was less than they had previously offered her, but it was a start. Sara's full-time job was to be Elizabeth's stage mother, accompanying her on set and defending her when she believed she needed it. She got paid from Elizabeth's wages for this. 10% of Elizabeth's gross earnings was taken and used to purchase war bonds in her name. According to a 1943 contract with MGM, the remainder of her salary "may be retained by said Elizabeth Taylor, and Francis Taylor and Sara Taylor, her father and mother, respectively." That kind of language provided child actors' parents a lot of discretion in terms of how much of their children's money they kept for themselves and how much they set aside for their kids.

Although Elizabeth had a minor role in Lassie Come Home, the film, which was made in color—still uncommon at the time—was a huge success, cementing her status as one of MGM's child stars. She would become the crown gem of the world's largest entertainment organization within a few years. The most important thing Elizabeth took away from the film was a lasting friendship with fellow British actor Roddy McDowall, who was the film's star and four years her senior. She returned to MGM to star opposite McDowall in The White Cliffs of Dover. The principal of Elizabeth's school then called Sara and informed her that she needed to find another school for Elizabeth to attend since she was becoming a distraction; the other students couldn't concentrate with her in class. This was an inconvenience for Sara, but it was also a clear indication that her daughter was on her way to becoming a legitimate movie star. Elizabeth's parents enrolled her in MGM School when she was ten years old, and she attended for the next eight years. It would be her only school experience. She felt alone going to school on set and being the only person in her grade at times. She was only allowed three hours of concentrated schooling per day, which had to be completed by 4:00 p.m. She wished she could go to a regular school where the learning was spread out over six hours and she could joke around with her pals.

Elizabeth was particularly taken with the lovely scent of the women's pancake makeup. She once summoned the nerve to approach Katharine Hepburn's table and request that she sign her autograph book, but Hepburn was preoccupied. "I was in such awe of her—she was one of the truly golden ones—that I became ice cold and white hot and began shaking." She was kind, but that was the last autograph I ever requested." They co-starred in Suddenly, Last Summer fifteen years later. Elizabeth imagined herself as the star of her own show, much like Danny Kaye in The Secret Life of Walter Mitty, a film in which he played a guy who led a monotonous life but cast himself as the hero of every story he imagined.

Years later, she reflected on how tough it was to be both a hugely successful figure and a student. "On the set, they would have a little black cubby hole where you could have your tutor for ten minutes at a time." So you had 10 minutes to memorize some information, then go out on the set, do your lines, come back, pick up where you'd left off, go out, slip back into character... It wasn't easy, and I'm not sure why we weren't all schizophrenics. Well, many of us were." MGM established "an artificial patriarchy" around Elizabeth, according to legendary director George Stevens, who directed her in "A Place in the Sun and Giant. "It replaced her own retiring father." The studio, like a controlling father, alternated between being severe and affectionate. All day, some authority told her what she should and should not do. She spent her whole preadolescent and adolescent days at Metro-Goldwyn-Mayer, with no opportunity to play and minimal interaction with other youngsters. She was escorted to a vacant room somewhere to study between takes." Of course, Elizabeth intuitively knew Stevens was correct—however unreasonable the expectations for female performers of her age were.

Sara's power was unbreakable before she married. Stevens recalls Sara saying things like "Elizabeth says" or "Elizabeth thinks" when Elizabeth was seated right next to her at lunch in the studio commissary. "I finally felt like shouting, 'Why don't you let Elizabeth say it herself?'" he said. Elizabeth attended pool parties organized by the studio or the parents of other stars so that photographers from fan publications like Photoplay and Movie Gems could photograph them. She'd forget about the cameras and take a deep dive into the water, emerging with water flowing out of her nose and laughing with delight. Russ Tamblyn, who played Elizabeth's younger brother in the 1950 film Father of the Bride, recalled teacher McDonald wearing her dark hair divided straight down the middle in a tight bun with her blouse buttoned all the way up to the top button. "She was very strict," Tamblyn explained, "and she watched over all of us and a bigger room with a ping pong table." Elizabeth, on the other hand, did not follow the same rules. "She was very independent, and she would talk back to Ms. McDonald," Tamblyn recalled. Elizabeth despised being considered as "a freak"; she wanted to go to college but couldn't since it would interfere with her work. Sara disregarded the possibility of applying to UCLA when she told her mother. "I'm sure all those girls going to UCLA wish they were Elizabeth Taylor." Russ Tamblyn recalls attending her lonely graduation party in the remote schoolhouse. Elizabeth celebrated her birthday cake with Tamblyn, as well as child actors Dean Stockwell and Jane Powell. Even with them, she felt out of place.

Elizabeth would go from being a talented young actress to a rare commodity with just one film. In the fall of 1943, producer Pandro S. Berman was looking for a beautiful little girl with a perfect English accent who could ride horses to play Velvet Brown, the main character in National Velvet, a film based on Enid Bagnold's 1935 bestselling novel. Berman had envisioned Katharine Hepburn in the major role years before, but she was now too elderly. The film is set in England between the two world wars, at a time when women's roles were limited and strictly defined. Her name was to be printed three times: once for her birth announcement, once for her wedding announcement, and once for her obituary. Women were not allowed to inherit property and could not vote in England until 1928 (the Nineteenth Amendment to the United States Constitution was enacted in 1920, although it did not apply equally to all women, and women of color were still barred from voting in many regions of the country for years). Elizabeth portrays Velvet, the daughter of a butcher in rural England who hopes to win a horse named The Pie in a village lottery.

When she wins The Pie, she fantasizes about riding her horse to victory in the Grand National Steeplechase, a horse race in which only male jockeys are permitted. Mickey Rooney, who was much more famous than Elizabeth at the time, plays the disillusioned jockey who assists Velvet in realizing her dream of winning the race by disguising herself as a boy—an exceedingly brave and daring gesture. Despite the fact that she is disqualified after it is found that she is a girl, Velvet is overtaken with pride knowing that she won the race. The film is about female empowerment and the decisions women must make between their goals and their families. It appeared to be a perfect match: Elizabeth's favorite novel was National Velvet, she had been riding horses since she was three years old, and she spoke with an English accent. And the narrative of a girl who defied the norms called to Elizabeth and her free-thinking, free-spirited outlook on life. But there was one seemingly insurmountable issue: Elizabeth was an eleven-year-old girl. She had the stature of a six- or seven-year-old. Every morning, Elizabeth ordered two Farm Breakfasts from Tip's, which featured two hamburger patties, two fried eggs, hash-brown potatoes, and silver-dollar pancakes. She rode her horse for an hour and a half every morning before school, she did forty jumps on her horse every day, and she swung from doorways in the hopes of growing taller.

She fell in love with King Charles, the grandsire of the famed racehorse Man o' War, who lived at the Pacific Palisades stables. Elizabeth was aware that he was a wild horse that had once jumped over a car, but he was her favorite and she urgently wanted to ride him. She'd crawl through an aperture in the hay bin up to the highest bale of hay at night to sit and talk to King Charles via a hole at the top of his pen's wall. She informed him she loved him and that she would try to cast him as The Pie. They were ecstatic to see that she had grown three inches. Sara saw it as part of God's plan—"there wasn't an atom of human will about it"—while Elizabeth saw it as proof of her own power. If she really wanted something, she'd find a way to get it. The story of how she acquired the position was woven into Elizabeth's life story, and Sara knew it would make fantastic copy.

In the film, Angela Lansbury played Velvet's older sister, and, like McDowall, she was taken aback by Elizabeth's attractiveness. Elizabeth's performance had an emotional vulnerability and depth that no other young performer matched. "I remember being dazzled by her extraordinary coloring, the violet blue eyes, the dark hair, the freckles, and the natural color in her cheeks, even at the time." She was the most beautiful little kid I'd ever seen." Despite this, the studio always saw opportunities for development. They intended to remove the mole on Elizabeth's right cheek that she later became famous for, as well as tint her luxuriant black hair because it appeared too dark on-screen. Her response was usually straightforward: No. The studio also wanted her hair cropped when she played Velvet, which Mickey Rooney did on-screen to help disguise her as a male jockey. Francis, who rarely spoke out, complained, and Elizabeth wore a short wig over her natural hair, which she tucked underneath. Elizabeth had also expressed her feelings on the subject, and chopping her long raven-colored hair into a boyish bob seemed unavoidable. The short wig was made for Elizabeth by MGM's head hairstylist, Sydney Guilaroff, who later became a personal friend of hers.

Francis and Sara also opposed when the studio sought to remove Elizabeth's prominent arched brows, which became a trademark of her appearance later on. There was even talk of changing her name to Virginia, which her parents dismissed. Francis stated unequivocally, "Take her as she is, or you don't get her at all." Sara was the ultimate definition of a stage mother, embodying all the positive and terrible traits of such a presence, such as defending her daughter at all times, and the relentless intrusion of herself into her daughter's life. She was genuinely experiencing life through Elizabeth. She would sit in the corner during filming and make elaborate hand gestures to Elizabeth while she was performing: if she put her hand on her stomach, Elizabeth's voice was too shrill; if she tapped her hand on her forehead, Elizabeth needed to stand up straighter and concentrate; if she placed her hand on her heart, Elizabeth was not delivering enough feeling in her performance; and if she placed her finger on her cheek, Elizabeth needed to stand up straighter and concentrate.

Elizabeth had no formal training other than her natural talent and Sara's guidance. There was a moment in which Pie was unwell and Velvet was caring for him all night. Velvet is supposed to cry when Mickey Rooney's character tells her that he doesn't think the horse will live. Rooney, who was twelve years Elizabeth's senior and a seasoned star, gave her some guidance. Instead of crying, Elizabeth, who already had a wicked sense of humor, began to laugh. She apologized and fled away when she couldn't stop herself. Elizabeth didn't need to make up a complicated story to cry. It just took her a few seconds to cry when she thought of King Charles dying. She was not a Stanislavski method actor like her famous friends Montgomery

Clift, James Dean, Paul Newman, and Marlon Brando. Elizabeth did not play a character both on and off film. Instead, she acted by putting herself in the shoes of the character she was portraying.

On her thirteenth birthday, the studio gifted her King Charles and a $15,000 bonus, which is worth more than $245,000 today. MGM wants to make an investment on its newest star. Elizabeth's weekly income increased from $200 to $750, with $250 going to Sara for chaperoning services. Elizabeth's rise to notoriety was lightning fast; it had taken the studio five years to turn Judy Garland into a star. Sara wished for Elizabeth's brother, Howard, to pursue a career in film as well. He was as attractive as Elizabeth was. But Howard was absolutely uninterested, which endeared him even more to his tiny sister. "He's completely un-superficial, totally unmaterialistic, the most real person I've ever known," she wrote. Sara wanted Howard to audition for a part in a Western when he was a teenager. He needed a new car and the only way to get one was to work. Jules Goldstone, Elizabeth's agent at the time, wanted to take Howard to 20th Century Fox for an audition.

Nobody ever mentioned acting to him again. Elizabeth admired Howard's renegade spirit and was even a little envious of him. Elizabeth had a horrible feeling about Louis B. Mayer from the start. She'd heard about how controlling he could be with his performers, and now she was witnessing it firsthand. Elizabeth learnt to stand up for herself in this no-holds-barred training field at the world's most brutal studio. She determined she would never wind up like Garland, 10 years her senior. Garland was tortured by MGM's rigorous edicts, which included restrictive diets, and as a young girl got hooked on medicines and cigarettes. Elizabeth, despite her youth, could see how MGM dominated over their most bankable performers. She regarded Mayer as the studio's "dictator" who "alarmed" her. There was a reason studio stars were referred to as a "stable." She claimed they were treated like animals and regarded studio property.

Norma Heyman, Elizabeth's best friend, met her on a film set in the 1960s and blamed Mayer for Elizabeth's lifelong addiction to medicines and drink. "I remember her telling me about the number of pills he'd [Mayer] make them take in the mornings so they'd be bright and chirpy, and another pill at lunchtime, and then pills she was supposed to take at home so she could sleep so she could get up at five a.m. to go back to the studio." If the studio required their stars, they had to ensure that their stars required them as well. And not just for financial gain. Mayer allegedly sanctioned not only the use of barbiturates (a common sleeping medicine that is rarely prescribed today due to the ease with which it can be overdosed), but also so-called "pep pills" (amphetamines). By the time she was seventeen and filming The Wizard of Oz, Garland had become an addict.

Mayer established the Department of Special Services, which served as the studio's public relations department. The stars' images were meticulously created by publicists. They encouraged Elizabeth to exhibit her love of animals after National Velvet, particularly her devotion for her pet chipmunk, Nibbles. The studio wanted gossip columnists and reporters to portray Elizabeth as a fresh-faced innocent; she would occasionally play jacks or jump rope in the front yard. The publicity department sent images of Elizabeth with her various pets to fan magazines. She formerly had eight chipmunks, a golden retriever, a cocker spaniel, a black cat, King Charles, and a squirrel as pets. Lassie Come Home and National Velvet benefited from her upbeat persona. She didn't mind because she clung to her pets as a memento of a childhood that had come to an end far too soon. But Elizabeth was much more than that; she possessed a dry wit from an early age. She wore a black velvet skirt and carried Nibbles on her shoulder to her first grownup cocktail party at the home of gossip journalist Louella Parsons. "Of course," she answered when asked if she liked animals, as they had read. I like people more than I enjoy people."

MGM sent Elizabeth to Washington for a White House event in 1946, when she was fourteen years old. They first scheduled a visit to a local children's hospital, where she sat with an eight-year-old kid who had been on an iron lung for more than a year. "He is so brave, and wonderful," she wrote. She then traveled to the White House, where she met First Lady Bess Truman at a March of Dimes event. She was dressed in her first fur coat, first black dress, and first pair of long stockings. "When we finally got there, it felt like butterflies or horses were prancing inside my tummy," she recounted. Despite her celebrity, Elizabeth was still a young girl who was not used to standing in dress shoes for extended periods of time. As Bess Truman sat at the front desk and Elizabeth sat behind her, there was a sea of cameras fixed on them. Sara stood behind the cameras in front of Elizabeth as the flashbulbs went off. She began indicating Elizabeth and pointing furiously at her feet. Because of the camera flashes, Elizabeth couldn't see her mother's desperate motions. She eventually noticed she was barefoot.

There was a gap between the release of Courage of Lassie and her return to the screen. During this time, Elizabeth traveled to MGM every day for school, interviews with reporters prescreened by studio publicists, lunch, and carefully arranged photographs. This brief hiatus from filmmaking was part of the studio's aim to assist her transition from child star to ingenue. Shirley Temple was unable to make a smooth transition, and the awkwardness of early adolescence had ruined many a child star's career. MGM was determined to control Elizabeth's appearance and keep any unattractive flaw, any embarrassing teen moment hidden. Sara and Francis were separated for four months in 1947. Francis was fed up with being excluded from his daughter's life. There were also reports that he had love relationships with men, which could explain Elizabeth's lifelong comfort with gay men. Francis married Sara when he was 29 years old; gay individuals were regarded mentally sick or dangerous in the 1920s, thus marriages of convenience were popular.

They finally reconciled, but Francis wanted to make a point. It didn't appear to stick. Whether Elizabeth liked it or not, Sara's choice to covertly remodel Elizabeth's bedroom on Elm Drive marked the beginning of Elizabeth's metamorphosis to womanhood. The studio was transforming Elizabeth into a teenage sex symbol, and her mother was helping them. Studio officials reasoned that by the time she was sixteen or seventeen, she would be ready to appear in another picture. They strategically issued stories over this time period to make her relevant. She was too young for marriage at the time, so they chose more wholesome narratives instead of giving her King Charles and releasing the book Nibbles and Me. The oddest decision was to give her a Ford convertible for her fourteenth birthday—two years before she was legally allowed to drive. Nothing was done by chance or without great thought and planning. Elizabeth was a far too valuable celebrity. To commemorate her seventeenth birthday in 1949, Life magazine released a full-length color portrait of her to demonstrate her maturation.

Elizabeth had been trained in the art of image creation since she was a child. "L.B. Mayer and MGM created stars out of tinsel, cellophane, and newspapers," she explained. When she was sixteen, she landed her first ingenue role in 1947's Cynthia. It was her first time wearing makeup in a movie and her first adult on-screen kiss. If spectators purchased tickets for the film, they would see Elizabeth experience her first real kiss. The phrase "Her First Kiss" was all over the movie posters. Of course, they were wrong, but it didn't matter because it was their way of reintroducing Elizabeth, this time as a full-fledged lady, even at fifteen. Elizabeth may have found a boy to kiss, but she was unable to find a boyfriend. She only knew folks from the studio lot, and she didn't know anyone her age at school. Sara's omnipresence frightened even the most daring suitor. Sara and Francis rented a Malibu beach house and organized parties, recognizing the importance of matching Elizabeth with someone she thought was suitable, but no one would talk to her.

Elizabeth questioned if she wanted to continue acting as she grew older. She and Sara battled about it all the time. Sara thought she had sacrificed her life for her ungrateful daughter, who now threatened to destroy it all. Elizabeth eventually capitulated and apologized, hoping to satisfy her mother. "My entire life has been in motion pictures," she wrote to her mother. Quitting would be like removing the roots of a tree—I'd quickly wilt and become lifeless and useless. Mom, I've made up my mind, and I swear I'll never, ever whine about being a very blessed girl again. And another thing—I've made a decision for myself to accept all of the trials and everything else that comes my way, because I know (and will always realize) that I was the one who chose to stay in—and that I'm the one who must accept them without moaning or wishing to quit." Sara was relieved, but she was still concerned about what people would think of Elizabeth's difficulty finding a boy to date. Elizabeth was invited to Roddy McDowall's birthday celebration, which was hosted by a fan magazine. Sara approached Bill Lyon, who was handling Elizabeth's publicity at the studio, and revealed the dilemma to him because she couldn't think of anyone to bring. But he couldn't find anyone since they were all too scared. Lyon ended up driving Elizabeth to the party. Elizabeth must have felt relieved after flirting with the world's biggest movie star. Elizabeth and Sara made a transatlantic cruise on the Queen Mary in 1947.

MGM publicists were putting pressure on Sara to find Elizabeth someone to date for PR purposes. And Elizabeth was plainly looking for love. The studio was not content with controlling what their stars wore; they also wanted to regulate how they lived their lives. And if an actor wanted to keep their work, they had no choice but to comply. If a celebrity stepped out of line, they were punished and money was deducted from their pay. Elizabeth's grownup knowledge was created in this ruthless world. In another unpublished interview with Meryman, Elizabeth described how, as a child performer, she witnessed more famous actors move bit players downstage and out of the spotlight so that they could shine "like a diamond in the royal crown setting." If you ventured to enter "that golden circle of light," where the primary star was standing, she warned, "you'd be cuffed behind the ears and you wouldn't even understand it." Elizabeth despised the treatment so much that when she got famous, she made it a point to do the opposite.

Elizabeth was observing and absorbing all of the cruelty and injustice that was going on around her, and she would never forget it. When she was fourteen, she and her mother went to Mayer's office to speak with him, or "Big Daddy," as she referred to him behind his back. Sara was informed that Elizabeth was being considered for a role in the film Sally in Her Alley. If the report was true, she'd have to start practicing right once because the part required singing and dancing, neither of which Elizabeth possessed. Elizabeth compared Mayer's office to Mussolini's. Visitors had to walk along a long white carpet to reach his office, where he sat at a white oak desk, admiring his subjects. Mayer was enraged that Sara would question him. If Elizabeth was interested in the part, he would let her know when he felt like it. As he grew white and rose up in rage, foam formed around the corners of his mouth as sweat poured down his cheeks.
Mayer never apologized to her and Elizabeth never once set foot in his office again. But she was not punished for her behavior. She was making MGM too much money.

Dore Schary arrived at the studio in 1948, and Mayer was preoccupied with retaining power. The movie industry was at its peak in 1946, but by 1953, the number of people attending the theater had dropped by nearly half as more and more Americans began purchasing televisions to watch at home. During the postwar economic boom, having a television in one's living room became a source of prestige. Mayer had left the company by 1951. Some of MGM's top stars, including Katharine Hepburn, Spencer Tracy, and Clark Gable, were also present. High-paid executives were forced to take pay cuts ranging from 25 to 50 percent every year, and MGM was resurrected for a brief period in the early 1950s. In 1947 and 1948, none of their films were nominated for Best Picture, but for the next six years, the company had a film nominated. Elizabeth, Grace Kelly, Ava Gardner, and Debbie Reynolds were among the final MGM stars standing by late 1955. Elizabeth witnessed the end of the so-called Golden Age, during which stars were cultivated, sculpted, and controlled.

Her former partner and companion George Hamilton remarked on how her childhood affected the course of her life in a 2021 interview. She felt manipulated by the studio, and perhaps more so by her parents. Being the breadwinner as a small child, according to Hamilton, caused her to mistrust her parents' reasons. Was her mother only adoring her because of the large sum of money she brought home every month? Russ Tamblyn recalled sitting between Elizabeth and Jimmy Stewart at the Beverly Hills premiere of That's Entertainment! in 1974. During the concert, someone approached Elizabeth and asked if she wanted to walk onstage with her dear friend Roddy McDowall and Lassie, and she declined. Nobody was going to force her to do something she didn't want to do. Never, ever again. It took Elizabeth decades to uncover the truth about why she consistently defied authority. And she never shared the full nature of it in public.

She called Francis one day in her early twenties and requested him to come to her house. She sat on his lap, wrapped her arms around him, and buried her head in his neck as they both grieved at the kitchen table. It was the first time they had truly connected since she was nine years old, when both of their lives were irrevocably changed. It was even worse than Elizabeth would confess publicly. Elizabeth told a close friend that her father had struck her in the jaw so hard that she suffered from TMJ, or lockjaw, for the rest of her life. She recounted Francis grabbing her hair and swinging her around the room in a violent rage before hitting her. It happened before Elizabeth went to work one morning. She explained it away, as she often did, by stating her father was embarrassed that Elizabeth was the family earner and that he felt emasculated. Her childhood humiliation and trauma were real, and they would follow her throughout her life, especially when she was subjected to physical and emotional violence by some of her relationships.

She never went to therapy, partly because it was not socially acceptable at the time, but also because she did not believe in focusing on bad memories; she was too concerned with the future. Instead, her life, like so many others, became a private struggle for control over her work, who she married, and how much of herself she was ready to share with the public. By the end, she had practically taken control of her own life. She could easily acquire money and give her mother the fame and fortune she had desired since she was a child, and she would care for her parents for the rest of their life.

CHAPTER 2
Love at a Young Age

By the time Elizabeth was sixteen, the studio and Sara had achieved success with their "glamor push." Elizabeth was in full bloom, with her luscious, velvet-black hair, crimson lips, and voluptuous five-foot-two frame. And they'd finally gotten her a date. Doris Kearns, Elizabeth's MGM publicist, and her husband asked if they might bring Glenn Davis, a handsome Heisman Trophy winner, to the Taylors' Malibu beach house. Davis, an army lieutenant, and his friend "Doc" Blanchard were cocaptains of the Army football team and were dubbed the "Touchdown Twins."

Publicists at the studio did everything they could to build interest in the lovely young couple. It felt like an out-of-body experience to Elizabeth. She knew she wouldn't marry him, but she went along with the story since it was beneficial for her career. Davis gave her his small gold football amulet, which she wore around her neck on a necklace. MGM dispatched Elizabeth to New York in October 1948 to have her portrait taken by acclaimed photographer Philippe Halsman in order to make the romance between her and Taylor more appealing to moviegoers. "You have bosoms," he exclaimed, "so stick them out!" The images were gorgeous, and it was at this point that she recognized her own power and capacity to shape her image—despite the fact that she was still a teenager. Michael Wilding, a thirty-six-year-old British actor, was in London at the same time Elizabeth was filming Conspirator for MGM. He used to come to Elizabeth's table in the commissary after lunch to converse with her. Sara was always nearby. "I noticed that every time he came in, Elizabeth's eyes lit up, as if by a slew of candles," Sara recalled. Without Glenn Davis, I knew Michael Wilding would be 'the man' in her life."

Then MGM ran into trouble with their Glenn Davis match. Elizabeth had fallen in love with someone else, and this was another occasion when she decided to fight back—at least initially. Elizabeth was on vacation with Sara on Miami Beach to celebrate her seventeenth birthday when she met millionaire William Pawley Sr., a former US ambassador to Brazil and aviation entrepreneur. She spent time by the pool with Pawley's kid, William, who had black hair and sparkling blue eyes. Their unexpected meeting in the spring of 1949 was her first true love experience. Elizabeth and Pawley exchanged over sixty letters between his house in Miami and hers in Los Angeles.

The issue was that Elizabeth was publicly dating Davis. She reveals the issue in her letters to Pawley. "It's been so bad since I got home, with all the reporters calling and asking if Glenn [Davis] and I had broken up." I didn't know what to answer at first, but we all talked it over and agreed to say, 'Well, we're not engaged, but we're still close friends and haven't broken up.' Elizabeth's letters show that she became increasingly frustrated with her double existence as the weeks passed. Davis was furious when she accidentally damaged a pair of earrings Pawley had given her. "I have never had such a strong desire to hit anyone with all my might in my life—I could just as easily have killed him," she wrote in a letter to Pawley.

Elizabeth and Pawley married when he was twenty-eight years old and she was seventeen. He was the first to present her with a diamond engagement ring. But it soon became evident that they had opposing views. The main issue was Pawley's desire for Elizabeth to leave the company. Sara was not going to let it happen, despite Elizabeth's interest in the notion. But she was quickly sidetracked by her most difficult performance yet, opposite Montgomery Clift in A Place in the Sun. The film is based on Theodore Dreiser's 1925 novel An American Tragedy, which tells the true story of a man who murders his pregnant factory-worker fiancée in order to marry someone from an affluent family. Dreiser's essay was a famed critique of materialism, and director George Stevens renamed the film A Place in the Sun, which was less depressing. Angela Vickers, a wealthy and gorgeous temptress, was played by Elizabeth. Angela Vickers achieved stardom as Velvet Brown, but she also established herself as a great actress. Stevens saw Elizabeth as "the girl on a candy box," a charming girl who may also be corrupt. Elizabeth was smitten by the script. Vickers was a spoiled affluent girl, but she had depth, especially when confronted with George's death sentence for murdering his lover.

Stevens began filming in Lake Tahoe in October 1949, when the water was frigid and Elizabeth often sat on set wrapped in a coat over her bathing suit. Every night, Elizabeth called Pawley, Florida, over the phone. Their engagement ended when he came to visit her in California, according to Sara. "I believe Elizabeth recognized for the first time how much she enjoyed being photographed. Not for the glamor, money, or enjoyment of it, but because it kept her connected to the world and people." Pawley called Elizabeth at her Bel Air house more than fifty years after their engagement ended to reminisce and possibly work his way back into her life. Pawley reflected on the forces that tore them apart in a heartfelt letter written on December 1, 2003. He wrote about Joe Schenck, the chairman of 20th Century Fox, predicting that MGM directors would never allow them to marry because Pawley had stated that he wanted Elizabeth to stop acting.

According to Pawley, when he showed Sara the engagement ring he planned to give Elizabeth, she urged him that he needed to propose straight away because "it will help us control who Elizabeth goes with." He proposed without even telling his family before the news was spread around the world. At 7:30 a.m. the next morning, Pawley heard a knock on the door of his father's house in Miami Beach and stepped downstairs in his bathrobe. He went along with the notion for a while, remembering how delighted they were when Francis offered to buy them any property they wanted on Miami Beach as a wedding present. "It seemed to me that our lives would be heavenly," he reflected. Schenck and his wife, perhaps feeling sorry for him, presented the news to Pawley over dinner at their home.

Elizabeth returned to California to film Father of the Bride, and her mother informed Pawley that there had been a change in plans, and Elizabeth would not be traveling to Miami. He needed to relocate to California if he wanted to marry her. But he didn't have a job in California, and the thought of Elizabeth assisting him made him uncomfortable. They had a fight two months before Elizabeth called off their engagement. Elizabeth begged Pawley's brother to tell Pawley how much she loved him in an 8-page letter. "When anyone even touches my arm or tries to take my hand, it just makes me shirk and want to run away, and I can't possibly conceive or imagine anyone else in this world but Bill." However, while they were engaged, he traveled to California to attend Jane Powell's wedding in 1949 and was taken aback when Powell stated, "Isn't it wonderful about Elizabeth's new contract?" "I had lost the love of my life, just as Joe Schenck had predicted." "The studio had triumphed!" He never married and had no children for twenty-five years. He'd never forgiven himself for failing to fight harder for Elizabeth. Pawley was simply adding another layer of control to her already overmanaged life. But there will come a moment when she will not seek approval from anyone.

CHAPTER 3
Bessie Mae

Elizabeth became absorbed in her work and a new transformative friendship. In many respects, Montgomery Clift, also known as Monty, was Elizabeth's mirror. They were both so stunning on-screen, Elizabeth with her oval face, deep blue eyes, heavy arched brows, and red bow lips, and Monty with his high cheekbones, green eyes, and thick dark hair. Monty, like Elizabeth, began acting as a child. He made his Broadway debut at the age of fourteen and was schooled in the Stanislavski style. He was the embodiment of a serious actor devoted to his craft, in contrast to Elizabeth, who had no formal training. He wore his dedication like a hair shirt. He primarily portrayed outcasts and loners, such as George Eastman. Monty appeared to be sullen and morose, with a sense of melancholy in his gaze. He despised Hollywood's trappings and rented a one-room bachelor flat with a Murphy bed.

Before A Place in the Sun began filming, Paramount executives felt that having Monty bring Elizabeth as his date to the opening of The Heiress, another Paramount film in which he starred, would be good marketing. Monty was well aware of the studio's tendency for pairing gay leading males with starlets in order to mask their sexuality. The charade's absurdity enraged him. He wanted to stay at his hotel and work on the writing for A Place in the Sun, but his agents said he couldn't. The studio wanted photographs of Elizabeth and Monty to pique the public's interest in their new film while also implying that they could be a pair. Monty was not in the mood to make small talk with a giggling, vacuous adolescent actress. The commodity, Elizabeth Taylor, embodied everything he detested about Hollywood. But he reluctantly agreed. When his limousine arrived at Elizabeth's house, she walked through the front door, dazzling in a white strapless gown with a full skirt. Sara wanted to see Monty inside the limo, but Elizabeth drew away from her mother.

He understood almost immediately when she took her seat in the vehicle that his new co-star was a foul-mouthed, funny, and intelligent force of nature. She was used to these black-tie gatherings and felt completely at ease. She placed her fur cover on the seat next to her and swore almost immediately. It was always unsettling to hear Elizabeth, who resembled a porcelain doll, swear. "I love four-letter words," she said, "they're so terribly descriptive." She and Monty were both self-deprecating and sarcastic, poking fun of themselves and others. "Why, you look absolutely lovely, Bessie Mae," Monty exclaimed, referring to her by a nickname he'd use for the rest of his life. He advised them to eat a hamburger before arriving for the premiere. Elizabeth was excited at the prospect of eating fast food in her evening gown. When they finally made their dramatic debut, they marched up to a radio announcer, past hundreds of admirers. Elizabeth took a time before the interview to straighten Monty's tie, already serving as a maternal figure in his life.

Aside from their physical attractiveness, she and Monty had a lot in common: they were both child stars with domineering mothers who understood the trappings of stardom. They could make each other laugh more than anything else. Elizabeth's relationship with Monty lasted longer than any of her previous marriages. Elizabeth would occasionally allow Monty to sit on the bathtub's edge, and instead of being distracted by her naked body, they would speak and laugh. She said she would have lost her virginity to him, and they were close, but he couldn't pull it off. Theirs was an eternally unattainable love, but she couldn't stop herself from wanting him. She liked to look at him and be with him, and while she was young enough to believe she could change him, she always knew who he was. It must have felt liberating for her to not have him focusing on her body and instead on who she was. (He did, however, tell his friends about her

31

"magnificent tits.") Monty did not feel guilty about his homosexuality, but he was frustrated by the fact that he had to disguise it, so he turned to drink. Gossip columnists, such as Hedda Hopper, were granted special access to gay celebrities on the condition that they not expose their sexuality to the public. It was an abhorrent type of blackmail. Monty was always aware that he would not be welcomed if he did not conform. So it was not surprising when Hopper wrote about Elizabeth and Monty's forthcoming marriage while they were filming, even if it was ludicrous.

A Place in the Sun took five months to complete, and it was the most difficult assignment of Elizabeth's acting career up to that moment. The film began filming before Father of the Bride, although it was not released until a year later. The famed director George Stevens was the most difficult on Elizabeth. He was known for viewing performers as manipulable puppets. He insisted on many retakes of her sequences with Monty, and when Stevens wasn't pleased, he would debate with Elizabeth until she exploded in rage. Even as a teenager, Stevens recognized Elizabeth's maternal impulses. She was accompanied on set by a social worker because she was not yet legally an adult. Elizabeth was surprised by the dialogue Stevens requested from her during the critical scene in which Angela and George confess their love for each other. Stevens was not going to modify anything, even though he realized that she felt foolish reciting the lines because she was so young. In New York, they liked to eat at Camillo's Restaurant, which was a favorite of Monty's. They had a quiet table in the back and bent over it conspiratorially until the restaurant closed. They once stayed so long that when the restaurant owner decided to paint the dining area, they offered to assist. They took off their shoes and eagerly picked up a set of paintbrushes. They painted until three a.m. It was just the type of mayhem they desired.

CHAPTER 4
"He Will Kill Her"

After Jane Powell's wedding, Elizabeth met the man who would become her first husband the same night she bid goodbye to Bill Pawley. Francis and Sara proposed that the wedding party travel to West Hollywood's Mocambo nightclub to hear Vic Damone perform. Elizabeth's eyes welled up with emotions as she sat with her parents at a cocktail table and Damone sang directly to her. Damone sat down next to Elizabeth after his set. The following day, the headlines read, "Off with the Old Love and On with the New." Conrad Nicholson "Nicky" Hilton Jr., the son of Hilton Hotels founder Conrad Nicholson, entered Elizabeth's life shortly after they met. Every week, the Hiltons and the Taylors enjoyed dinner at the Hiltons' Bel Air mansion and the Taylors' Beverly Hills residence. Sara stated, "We couldn't have liked Nick any more." And Sara had to agree that Elizabeth marrying into a fantastically wealthy and distinguished family was a good thing.

Elizabeth and Hilton announced their engagement a week before her sixteenth birthday. Elizabeth needed to be persuaded to wait that long. When reporters pressed her for further information, she replied, "We both love hamburgers with onions, oversized sweaters, and Pinza." (Ezio Pinza was an opera singer from Italy.) It was a shaky basis for a relationship. Elizabeth called Monty in New York to tell him about her new love. She mocked him with it, but it didn't change the truth that Monty would never desire her the way she wanted him. "We're engaged," she announced, intending to make him envious. "What do you think?" Monty was at a loss for words. He was concerned since he had heard that Hilton was violent when he drank. "Nothing, Bessie Mae, except, are you sure Nicky Hilton is the right man for you?" Monty poured himself a huge glass of Jack Daniel's with ice and threw it down once he hung up the phone. It was her second booking, and she had already starred in almost 10 films. Even with all of her experience, and possibly because of the cloistered culture she grew up in, Elizabeth had no idea what she was getting herself into.

A fiery young woman needed to be tamed in mid-twentieth-century Hollywood. In the eyes of the public, she had broken the hearts of Glenn Davis and Bill Pawley, and in such a fervently puritanical era, people needed to be convinced that she was a virgin, a "good" girl. Sara, on the other hand, had reservations about her daughter's virginity. Elizabeth was taken to a doctor just before her wedding to Hilton for a treatment to open her hymen. Sara wished to open Elizabeth's hymen so that sex would be less unpleasant the first time. She also had a hidden agenda: she wanted to ensure that her daughter remained a virgin. According to Elizabeth's secretary Jorjett Strumme, who worked for her in the 1980s and early 1990s, the unethical virginity test lingered with her her entire life. Elizabeth claimed to be a virgin "not only physically, but also mentally." On April 1, 1949, she wrote in a 10-page letter to Pawley, "If only I could find the words that tell of that much love—so I could let you know how I feel." I guess I'll simply have to wait till I'm your wife to show you and prove my love for you." She concluded with astounding foresight about how much she would like makeup sex. It was common opinion that a true woman should save herself for marriage, and this influenced the rest of Elizabeth's life. It also led her down the aisle eight times because she was instructed not to sleep with a guy she loved until she married him (though she succumbed to temptation frequently later in life).

The wedding took place on May 6, 1950, one month before the film's debut and two months after Elizabeth turned eighteen. The event, conducted at the Beverly Hills Roman Catholic Church of the Good Shepherd, drew 700 guests, including MGM stars Fred Astaire, Ginger Rogers, and Esther Williams. The ceremony was followed by a banquet at the Bel Air Country Club. Elizabeth walked down the aisle wearing a 4-carat diamond ring, which was far less than the jewels her following husbands would give her, but still a substantial stone. Her outfit was designed by her friend, Academy Award-winning MGM costume designer Helen Rose, and had a sweetheart neckline covered in a chiffon overlay. Their honeymoon was also a show. They were greeted by a crowd at Los Angeles International Airport before flying to Chicago, where they picked up a Cadillac and traveled to New York. The automobile was loaded onto the Queen Mary in order for them to use it on their extensive European trips. Elizabeth traveled with seventeen pieces of luggage, a personal maid, and a poodle that had been colored to match the color of her eyes. When waiters mistakenly addressed Hilton as "Mr. Taylor," he reacted angrily. She did not always attain her desired outcome. The Duke and Duchess of Windsor, one of the only other celebrity couples to rival Taylor and Hilton's, had previously reserved the bridal suite.

Their honeymoon in Europe was supposed to last five months, but it only lasted two weeks. That's when Hilton began drinking again. He spent the majority of the day drinking and gambling, leaving Elizabeth alone in their hotel room to mourn and chain-smoke. Sara decided to write the first authorized biography of her daughter's life at the age of eighty-six in order to "tell the truth about Elizabeth and the reasons for or causes of the heartbreaking failures of her [then] five marriages." Although it was never published, Sara's handwritten notes demonstrate how much she knew about Hilton and his reputation. Everything seemed normal for the first few days of their trip, and Elizabeth sent pleasant postcards to her relatives. The postcards then ceased arriving, and there was a deafening quiet. "While in Paris, Elizabeth wrote us a beautiful letter in which she expressed her gratitude for all the years of love, kindness, and devotion we have shown her." That was the final letter she sent us."

Newspapers quickly began publishing early warning signs of disaster.

Elizabeth insisted that she was alright when her parents called. "You know the first year is the most difficult. We'll figure it out. Please don't be concerned." However, when they returned to New York in late August, Elizabeth was a shell of her former self. She'd dropped twenty pounds. Elizabeth realized she couldn't stay married to Hilton any longer. Back in Los Angeles, she stayed at her agent's home and at the home of her stand-in, Margery Dillon, but not at her parents'. Sara's notes suggest that she was either unaware of or unable to accept her daughter's pain. True, she didn't want to appear to be running home to her parents, but she also didn't want to listen to her parents advise her to struggle through an unworkable marriage. One of the worst things that might have happened had actually occurred, and she had no idea how far Hilton's cruelty could go. During their honeymoon, Hilton had kicked her in the tummy, causing her to miscarry. Elizabeth opted to divorce seven months after their wedding day, in early December. It was her first important decision on her own. But the further she pushed him away, the more he desired her. He unexpectedly came up at friends' residences where she had sought safety. He sent her roses and begged her to accept him back.

The last straw took place when she was with Hilton and her parents at her Uncle Howard's Connecticut estate when they were still married but no longer living together. She was appalled at the idea of divorce, especially after less than a year of marriage, but she knew that there could be no chance of reconciliation. She was sitting with Hilton alone in the living room as he begged her to take him back. She did not ask for alimony. All she wanted was her freedom, which she was learning was priceless. On December 14, 1950, the legal department at MGM released a statement on Elizabeth's behalf. "I am very sorry that Nick and I are unable to adjust our differences, and that we have come to a final parting of the ways. We both regret this decision, but after personal discussions we realize there is no possibility of a reconciliation."

On January 29, 1951, the divorce was granted. Her first marriage ended after eight months. It was a whirlwind nightmare that began sixty-eight days after her eighteenth birthday and ended twenty-nine days before she turned nineteen. After the divorce, Elizabeth was homeless and consumed with anxiety. She would not go back to live with her parents, and not only because she worried about the public perception that she was running home to her mother, but because she had tasted freedom and was not willing to part with it just because of one, albeit huge, mistake. Her agent, Jules Goldstone, suggested that she hire a secretary-companion and put her in touch with Peggy Rutledge, a woman who had once worked for Bob Hope's wife, Dolores. They met in Goldstone's office.

In March 1951, they moved into a five-room furnished apartment on Wilshire Boulevard. It was a month and a half after her divorce from Hilton, and Elizabeth was free from her mother's suffocating control and her husband's violence. But the trauma of the abuse led to a severe case of colitis, and she was ordered by her doctors to eat nothing but baby food. At that moment, she needed a sympathetic ear and found it in Stanley Donen, the director of her new film, Love Is Better Than Ever. But the studio—and her mother—were not happy. Donen was Jewish and therefore, in Sara's mind, off-limits. He was also still married, though he was separated from his wife. Sara made it clear to Elizabeth that Donen, who was the acclaimed director and choreographer of On the Town and Singin' in the Rain, was not fit to be her second husband.

Elizabeth and Donen remained uncomfortably close after the filming was finished. The studio determined that, no matter how much Elizabeth felt about him, they needed to protect her from herself and play the card they had been keeping. "We agreed that the best way to separate them was to send her abroad to make a picture," one executive explained. "She got the role of Rebecca in Ivanhoe and left for London that June." During this brief period, she also found herself in the unusual position of being the subject of an FBI investigation. She'd gotten an anonymous phone call threatening to explode in her hotel room. When she was not there, the FBI searched her hotel room for a device. If the caller contacted again, she was instructed to have someone else in the suite pick up the second phone and call the FBI agent on the switchboard. Her duty was to keep the suspect talking so they could track him down. Monty was in the living room when the phone rang, and he dashed into the bedroom to call the authorities. Elizabeth stayed on the phone for twenty minutes while the man explained what he wanted to do to her and how he planned to murder her in filthy terms. Finally apprehended, he was taken to Bellevue Hospital for psychiatric evaluation and diagnosed with schizophrenia.

Later, during a break from filming Ivanhoe, she was flying from London to the south of France in an eight-passenger plane when she had the unusual feeling that someone's eyes were looking hard at the back of her head. She saw the same man everywhere for the next few days. He even insisted on purchasing her a bottle of champagne at one point. The cops discovered charts with dates and times recording who she had been with and where she had gone in his motel room. He was imprisoned for several months before being deported to England. But he had tracked her down while she was on vacation. She never heard from him again, but his menacing message stayed with her. The episode occupies numerous pages of Elizabeth's 154-page FBI file. It's full of threats, including emails from people begging her to pay them money, some threatening to harm her, and many referring to her as a "whore."

One note, sent in 1949, when she was only seventeen years old, accused her of behaving like "the girl who hangs around bars and lets men get what they want out of her." Several guys have been arrested for stalking her over the years. When Elizabeth was a teenager, police promised her protection, and her parents were urged to keep a revolver in their car's glove compartment. She knew she was a product that could make all kinds of people rich—agents, producers, studio executives—but she also lived in fear of becoming a target for violence. Jorjett Strumme claimed Elizabeth told her about a man who had written to her, threatening to dismember her in the manner of "the Black Dahlia," an aspiring actress who was brutally killed. Fame came at a hefty cost. Following her divorce from Hilton, Howard Hughes saw an opportunity to finally persuade Elizabeth to fall in love with him. He devised an intricate plan this time: he knew she was staying at a house in Palm Springs as she tried to regain her footing after the divorce. She wore a wet towel over her swimming suit while sunbathing by the pool with some pals. She was startled to hear the humming of a helicopter as it landed roughly on the lawn, blowing leaves off the palm trees. Hughes got outside and walked over to Elizabeth's side. Greg Bautzer, Hughes's lawyer, once called Elizabeth and asked whether she would consent to marry Hughes, and she burst out laughing. Hughes was in love with her, according to Bautzer, and he insisted that Hughes was serious. What did she require him to prove to her? A knock came on the door of Elizabeth's hotel suite two hours later. When she answered the door, there stood a man clutching two suitcases full of cash. Elizabeth picked up the phone and dialed Bautzer's number. Hughes may have irritated her, but she never missed an opportunity to remind the men in her life about his hard efforts. According to Elizabeth's seventh husband, John Warner, Elizabeth enjoyed rehashing Hughes' obsession with her. She would ridicule Warner after their divorce, saying, "Howard Hughes offered me two million dollars to marry him, and I didn't get a dollar out of you!"

CHAPTER 5
Marriage and Love

When Elizabeth reconnected with the gorgeous British actor Michael Wilding while working in London, she was still weak and on a diet of pureed food to cure the ulcers and colitis she had suffered following her marriage to Hilton. Wilding had been her crush since she was sixteen. She informed her father how amazing Wilding had been to her throughout the filming of Ivanhoe and how much they shared, "just like you and mother." She saw Wilding, who was twenty years her senior, as a safe haven, a "oasis." He looked across the table at her one evening at dinner in Los Angeles and remarked, "Darling, you should wear sapphires to match your eyes." She took him with her the next morning to look at some sapphire engagement rings she had her eye on. When she showed her mother her sapphire engagement ring, they both sobbed. She had already lived a lifetime at the age of twenty, and she was not going to let Wilding go.

On February 21, 1952, they married in a ten-minute ceremony at London's Caxton Hall Registry Office. Helen Rose designed Elizabeth's wedding gown once more, but this time it was significantly different from the beautiful and traditional white gown she wore to her first wedding. She donned a gray wool suit with white organdy sleeves this time. The low-key wedding was a statement that she was taking a new approach to this marriage. Even if she tried to keep it hidden, as was always the case with Elizabeth, it could never be normal. Three thousand people waited outside for the new newlyweds to appear. When they did, one ecstatic fan snatched her cap from her head. Elizabeth had to be carried up and pushed through the mob into the vehicle to take her to their little wedding reception at Claridge's, where only fourteen guests were invited. They took a short honeymoon in Switzerland before returning to work.

Back in Los Angeles, she and Wilding purchased a two-bedroom ranch house on top of a mountain for $75,000 ($800,000 in today's currencies). To her great relief, she became pregnant quickly (contrary to what the doctor predicted), and she worked until she was five months pregnant, doing her best to disguise it from the director and producers of her next picture, The Girl Who Had Everything, because she knew she would be penalized for it. She revealed her pregnancy as soon as she concluded filming in 1952. She was promptly suspended, as she had predicted. Wilding was a successful leading actor in England, but when he arrived in California, he signed with MGM and struggled to find employment.

Elizabeth was under a lot of financial pressure, and she was dealing with a lot of misogyny. "I recall going down on my knees before an executive at MGM who shall remain nameless. I was married to Michael Wilding and pregnant when I was suspended. We had purchased a home and desperately needed $10,000 to avoid foreclosure. I pleaded with him to lend me $10,000. But she ignored her frustration and fury and focused on her pregnancy. "I was completely idiotic with pride when I was pregnant." You'd think I was the only woman who had ever conceived and carried a child... I've never felt so lovely." Michael Howard Wilding was born via Cesarean section at Santa Monica Hospital on January 6, 1953. Elizabeth had to return to work. Elizabeth and the other stars, including actor Peter Finch, were seated in a Jeep while a wind machine blasted air at them while shooting publicity photos for the forgettable 1954 picture Elephant Walk. Something struck her right eye as her hair blew delightfully. She felt a horrible scratching feeling every time she blinked. She was told she had a "foreign object" in her eye when she went to visit a doctor. "Anybody I know?" she asked, trying to make light of her situation.

During the weeks she spent healing, she pondered retiring. She expected to be offered more challenging roles after A Place in the

Sun, but instead found herself typecast as the pampered rich girl in a string of forgettable flicks. She determined that she desired more and would find a method to obtain it. Being the world's most renowned actress and a mother was a difficult balancing act for Elizabeth, no matter how hard she tried. "A part of me regrets becoming a public utility," she admitted. She would later apologize to her adult children for not being around as often as she would have liked after a few drinks. She was concerned about the consequences of her celebrity, her several marriages, and their wandering lifestyle. She fell pregnant with her second kid when Michael was one year old. The couple decided they wanted a larger home and located the "most beautiful house," according to Elizabeth, in the Hollywood canyons overlooking Los Angeles and the Pacific Ocean in the distance. The architect intended the owners to feel as if they were outside in nature. The living area had floor-to-ceiling windows that looked out into the pool, which had rock formations in it. There was a bark wall covered in orchids, mosses, and ferns. Sara informed Elizabeth that the architect, a family friend, had created it with Elizabeth in mind. She simply had to have it.

Christopher Edward Wilding was born on February 27, 1955, his mother's birthday. A golden retriever, a wirehaired foundling, two poodles, four cats, King Charles (her beloved horse from National Velvet), and a duck whose favorite location in the house was perched on Elizabeth's shoulder were among the family's pets. Unlike other ladies her age, Elizabeth was never trained to cook or clean since she didn't need to. She had everything she wanted materially when she was a child. She also did not perform any housework. She grew up with nannies and housekeepers who took care of her. Never mind that she was one of the highest-paid actresses at the time, and that she was mostly responsible for sustaining her growing family. Her unwillingness to throw her dirty clothing in the hamper irritated him. Her incompetence, or disinterest, in being on time was the one consistent feature that stayed throughout her life. She was constantly late, whether it was to meet a head of state or to take her wedding vows. Elizabeth's persistent and chronic tardiness—often hours late to the set, a dinner party, or even boarding a plane—was due in part to her excessive "Walter Mittying," or daydreaming. When she had no one her own age to talk to at school on the MGM lot, she developed a deep inner life out of necessity. Then there was the pressure to always be immaculate.

If the studio requested her to do something, her rebellious nature would emerge, and she would do whatever to avoid pleasing them. Being late and being unwell were sometimes the only cards she had. She eventually followed Humphrey Bogart's counsel and asserted herself more with Wilding. Their disagreements became more regular. Wilding was a British gentleman who was not the domineering lover she desired. She wanted someone powerful and equal to her, not someone who told her what to do just because he could. Hilton had attacked her, and the men she married after him were sometimes physically abusive as well; she frequently hit them back. Wilding, on the other hand, was not one of those men. She chose confrontations with him in which only Elizabeth screamed, and there was no passionate makeup sex, which she needed. "I'm not your child." "I'm your wife!" she exclaimed. She was stronger than she had been after her divorce from Hilton; she didn't need Wilding anymore, and he couldn't tolerate it. Eddie Fisher, who later married Elizabeth, claimed that she was unhappy and dissatisfied with Wilding. She had abandoned the old-fashioned expectation of waiting for marriage before having sex by that point.

Wilding and his siblings, Michael and Liza, were approximately ten years old when they chose to go skating on a little ice rink belonging to the local school they were attending in Gstaad, Switzerland, where Elizabeth had a residence in the 1960s (a house she kept as a shelter for decades). They were passing past the usual photographers camped out at the bottom of the driveway when they realized one of them had decided to follow them. We tried our best to ignore this unwanted presence, but it was tough; the situation was awkward. He just stood there staring at us, not even snapping shots. I fell and split my chin on the ice when I slipped. There was a lot of blood, and tears were unavoidable. Suddenly, the photographer took up his camera and began clicking furiously. It was really humiliating, and I was flushed with humiliation and rage. The fact that this parasitic voyeur—a stranger!—had calmly waited to profit from my exposed sorrow made me feel personally betrayed and abused, as if this man had broken and breached some sort of unspoken taboo. This episode resonated with me because it affected me personally and was one of those individual bricks that eventually became the wall separating childhood and maturity."

Decades later, the same photographer approached Wilding outside a hotel near Michael Jackson's Neverland Ranch, where his mother had married construction worker Larry Fortensky. Back in his hotel room, Wilding opened the package and took out a black-and-white 8 x 10-inch snapshot of himself as a ten-year-old, standing on a skating rink, holding back tears and using a mittened hand to stop the bleeding from a serious gash on his chin. "I'm intrigued that the photographer thought this 'gift' would create a positive point of connection between him and myself, or that it might grant him special access to the upcoming nuptials." It only brought back the terrible recollection. Elizabeth's sons frequently returned home with black eyes and bloody noses to protect her from classmates who ridiculed them about their stunning sex-symbol mother. Elizabeth wished to believe they were undamaged, even knowing the stress they were under. She wasn't the mother she wished to be, and she knew one day they'd discover how different their lives were from everyone else's. She did, however, partake in the fantasy while they were little.

CHAPTER 6
Rock, Jimmy, and Monty

Angela Lansbury, who played Elizabeth's sister in National Velvet, was blind to the studio's power over Elizabeth. "She made the transition so effortlessly because MGM supported her throughout those years," she explained. "Suddenly she appeared, and there she was... She simply took off, like a lovely bird." In reality, Elizabeth felt like a prisoner. Between A Place in the Sun and The Last Time I Saw Paris, she appeared in a string of films that were beneath her acting ability: Love Is Better Than Ever and Ivanhoe in 1952, The Girl Who Had Everything in 1953, and Rhapsody, Elephant Walk, and Beau Brummell in 1954. A journalist questioned Elizabeth in an unreleased interview how being renowned at such a young age made her think differently about her job than an actress who makes it in her twenties. Her response was telling. Despite her hard work, she described her performance in National Velvet as "accidental." A spate of negative film reviews following National Velvet hurt, but they did not destroy her.

She landed the part of matriarch Leslie Benedict in the epic film that reunited her with George Stevens, who had directed her in A Place in the Sun, despite living in a condition of continual struggle to acquire what she desired. She knew Stevens wanted Grace Kelly, so she worked hard to persuade him that casting her instead would not be a mistake. She had feelings of "hero worship" for him. The multigenerational drama was based on Edna Ferber's best-selling novel of the same name and spanned three decades. It presented the narrative of how a prosperous Texas family's wealth shifted from cattle to oil. Elizabeth, who was twenty-three at the time, plays a fifty-year-old woman who is the mother of Dennis Hopper, who is nineteen. In 1955, on the set in Marfa, Texas, she became good friends with Rock Hudson and James Dean, whom she referred to as

"Jimmy." The bonds she developed with Rock and Jimmy were more important to Elizabeth than her touching portrayal of a woman who urges her husband to improve the conditions on their ranch for the primarily Mexican-American crew. Jimmy, who was quiet and devilishly gorgeous, piqued her interest. And she and Rock hit it off right away, slipping off the set alone and whispering to each other like toddlers on a playground.

Rock was constantly threatened by magazines like Confidential exposing his sexuality. His unexpected marriage to his manager's assistant, Phyllis Gates, who claimed she had no knowledge Rock was gay, was the only way to calm suspicions that may ruin his lucrative profession. When they separated three years later, in 1958, Gates recalled Rock's control over her during the court hearing. It was a situation that had been played out hundreds, if not thousands, of times before. Physical abuse was not devastating to Rock's career at the time, but disclosing his sexuality would have been. When they weren't needed on the site, Rock and Elizabeth would sneak away to drink tequila in Ojinaga, a village near the United States' border with Mexico, which Elizabeth could relate to.

They told each other everything and stayed up late talking about it. When the hail was the size of golf balls, Elizabeth and Rock raced outside and gathered some to use in a new drink: the chocolate martini, which was made with ice, vodka, Hershey's syrup, and Kahla. Elizabeth remembers it as the most delectable drink she'd ever had. Jimmy and Rock did not get along, despite the fact that they both loved Elizabeth and vied for her attention. Jimmy, like Monty, was a technique actor, and Rock, like Elizabeth, was more of an instinctual performer. According to Rock's wife, Phyllis, before they even started shooting, Rock was jealous of Jimmy. He didn't mind that Jimmy had a smaller part than he did. The film's star was Rock, who played Jordan "Bick" Benedict Jr., the ranch's owner. Jimmy portrayed local rancher Jett Rink, who becomes wealthy after discovering oil. When they began filming, Rock quietly grumbled that Jimmy was getting all the close-ups. Jimmy was a year older than Elizabeth, who was twenty-three, and five years younger than Rock. He had sandy-blonde hair, a chiseled face, and a very seductive smile. He radiated mystery, which complemented his good appearance.

Jimmy, twenty-four, enjoyed driving his Jeep out into the desert alone and hunting jackrabbits. On set, he wore his Stetson hat low over his eyes and spoke in the Texas drawl taught to him by ex-rodeo star Bob Hinkle. He idolized Monty, which made acting alongside Monty's buddy Elizabeth all the more difficult. Elizabeth cared for Jimmy in a different, more maternal way than she did for Rock. She felt the same way about Monty that she needed to take care of him. What he told her was awful. She revealed what they were discussing to writer Kevin Sessums, but she made him agree not to publish it until after she died. "When Jimmy was eleven years old and his mother died, he began to be molested by his minister." That, I believe, tormented him for the rest of his life. In fact, I'm very sure it did. We discussed it extensively. We'd stay up late talking about Giant, and it was one of the things he disclosed to me." Elizabeth's friendships with Monty, Jimmy, and Rock assisted her in redefining her life's purpose decades later. They were her employees, confidants, and closest pals.

Filming Giant was a huge professional challenge for Elizabeth. Stevens was Elizabeth's idol, but he was tough to deal with. He demanded numerous retakes, announced production halts until he worked out a solution to a perceived problem, and he never accepted subpar performances. When Stevens concluded shooting A Place in the Sun, he brought home four hundred thousand feet of film, the most of which was cut. On the set of Giant, though, he pushed Elizabeth too far. Stevens, she claimed, was a bully who alternated between picking on Elizabeth and Jimmy. Jimmy once went on strike for three days following a disagreement with Stevens. Elizabeth had her own issues when she arrived at the Giant set. She was fatigued after a second Cesarean section to give birth to her second son, Christopher, and she was worried about the state of her marriage to Michael Wilding. She felt an undercurrent of second-guessing and contempt for her acting choices on set. Stevens screamed in front of the entire team when she informed him she thought her wardrobe for one scene was too casual and unlike anything her character would wear.

To demonstrate that she was weighing in on a creative decision that had nothing to do with how she appeared in the picture, she removed all of her makeup and knotted her hair in an untidy ponytail with a rubber band. They performed the scene, both of them defeated. On set, her back was giving her a lot of discomfort, and Stevens assumed it was all in her head. Later, after Elizabeth married Mike Todd and underwent back surgery, Mike sent Stevens X-rays of her spine as a Christmas card to demonstrate that her agony was genuine. The most dramatic confrontation occurred in the spring of 1955, when Elizabeth's character, Leslie Benedict, left her abusive husband's ranch in Texas and returned to her family's home in Maryland. She is the maid of honor during her sister's wedding, and the moving scene depicts her standing next to the bride, feeling her husband, played by Rock, standing behind her. He's returned to apologize, and when the vows are read, it's as if the two of them are reaffirming their own. The characters do not speak, but their eyes transmit a complex blend of shame, sadness, and love.

She cried again not long after, this time over a heartbreaking personal loss. On September 30, 1955, it was late at night, and Stevens, Elizabeth, and other cast members were seeing rushes in the Warner Brothers projection room. Stevens answered the phone when it rang. "No—my God!" he cried out. "When? "Are you certain?" Stevens hung up the phone, paused the movie, and turned on the lights. "I've just learned that Jimmy Dean has been killed," he added. Nobody said anything. It didn't make any sense. Jimmy had been in Marfa for four days, finishing out his final sequences. Jimmy was just twenty-four years old, but he was important. Elizabeth had just given him a Siamese kitten as a farewell gift, and she had been the last person on the set with Jimmy before he left.

Stevens called Elizabeth the next morning and demanded that she return to work and finish a scene. She claimed her eyes were puffy from sobbing all night. He remained unfazed. She went along with it because she was used to being told what to do by directors and studio officials. But it didn't mean she wasn't going to call him out on it. When the scenario was over and she could go home for the day, she screamed at Stevens, "You are a callous bastard!" When Giant was first released, it was billed as "a story of big things and big feelings." It was a critical and economic triumph, and Stevens received his second Academy Award nomination for directing. The film, which was decades ahead of its time, deftly takes on topics of racism, class conflict, and gender inequity. Jimmy's efforts were recognized. "It is James Dean who gives the most striking performance and creates in Jett Rink the most memorable character in Giant," the New York Times stated. Dean embodied the postwar young rebel who smoked and dressed in leather jackets and blue denim. The sole film made before John Steinbeck's death was East of Eden, based on his famous novel. Subsequent films, such as Rebel Without a Cause and Giant, cemented his legacy. He had the same good looks as Clark Gable and Cary Grant, but he was frail and melancholy. "You're an odd one, aren't you?"

In Giant, Elizabeth's character says. To Elizabeth, he would always be the young kid she wished to protect. Elizabeth's marriage to Wilding was still falling apart. She organized a leisurely dinner party to take her mind off her personal situation not long after she finished shooting Giant. On May 12, 1956, she called Monty and pleaded with him to come, but he refused. Finally, she forced him to do it.

Monty had rejected Hollywood's studio system by refusing to sign a long-term deal because he knew it would imprison him, just as Elizabeth had. In Red River, The Search, From Here to Eternity, and I Confess, he opted to play strange characters. He and Elizabeth were traveling back and forth to Danville, Kentucky, where they were filming Raintree County, a Civil War drama that MGM hoped would be the 1950s equivalent of Gone with the Wind. Monty was disappointed in the three-hour version of Ross Lockridge Jr. 's 1948 Civil War novel, which was not as gripping as the American classic. Producers hoped it would recreate some of the magic that existed between Elizabeth and Monty in A Place in the Sun, but the writing fell far short. Elizabeth stated she thought filming was going well, despite collapsing from the heat and her seventy-five-pound corseted antebellum costume. The night of Elizabeth's dinner party was misty, and Monty despised driving in the dark to Elizabeth's residence in Beverly Hills, off Benedict Canyon. Even in broad daylight, the small canyon road proved perilous. Monty's old friend, actor Kevin McCarthy, was present, as was Rock and his wife, Phyllis. Elizabeth appeared from her bedroom a half-hour late, glowing in a white satin cocktail gown. She sat on the sofa next to Monty and spoke in whispers. Michael Wilding was on another sofa, attempting to relieve a back spasm.

Elizabeth understood Monty like no one else. "He was a very quiet person and bashful," Saint recalled. "Before we were scheduled to shoot our first love scene together, I invited him to lunch. I wanted us to get together and to feel more at ease. Well, lunch was awkward as we ate in silence, and he never said a word. However, after lunch we filmed our first love scene, and he was wonderful. As long as we were in character, Monty felt comfortable." In a recent interview, Saint says that she did not think that Monty was openly gay at the time of making Raintree County. "If the actors I worked with felt they had to hide their sexuality, I wasn't aware of this. It wasn't discussed." And that was the issue; it was so deeply hidden that it was not acknowledged, even off-camera. At dinner Elizabeth talked about the beautiful costumes the designers had made for her for Raintree County. Even the petticoats were being made with the best material. "All they'll see is your tits, darling," Monty said. After dinner he excused himself to use the restroom. Monty did not drink much that night, but when he went into the bathroom a little after midnight he took some downers. He hoped they would help him fall asleep once he got home. But when he came out of the bathroom he was glassy-eyed. When Wilding asked him how he was feeling, Monty replied, "None too gorgeous."

McCarthy was getting ready to leave, too, and Monty asked if he could follow him down the winding canyon road to Sunset Boulevard. McCarthy sensed something was wrong immediately as they made their way down the dark twisting street: "He was following me, and he'd come up behind me very fast and very close to my bumper—and these roads were treacherous. His lights were coming up awfully close. At first, I thought that he was pulling a prank, trying to bump into my car. It was the kind of thing he would do. . . . I was afraid for him, but I was afraid for myself too. If he were to bump me, my car could easily tumble off the road. After he made the second sharp turn, McCarthy waited for Monty. "Suddenly, I heard a crash. Monty's lights were no longer in my rearview mirror, but I could see a cloud of dust. I turned my car around and drove back one hundred yards or more, where he was." Monty's car had hit a telephone pole. In the pitch black the smell of gas hung in the air. McCarthy got out of his car and at first he could not see Monty. He reached through the broken window and turned off the ignition, afraid that the car would blow up. He strained to see a figure slumped in the front seat. Monty's body was under the dashboard. "I was terrified he might be dead," McCarthy said. He couldn't open the door, so he got back in his car and drove to Elizabeth's house.

Back at the house, Rock and Phyllis were having a glass of brandy with Elizabeth and Wilding. McCarthy rang the doorbell. Elizabeth, Michael, Rock, and Phyllis raced to their cars in the driveway and went down the hill, where they found Monty's car, which had turned into a heap of smashed metal. McCarthy had already called an ambulance, and without hesitating, Elizabeth tried prying the car door open herself. She was always running toward danger and devastation, never away from it. The driver's-side door was jammed, so she opened the back door and crawled into the front seat, where she sat next to him. "His face, so handsome minutes before, was now a pulpy mask," Phyllis wrote. Elizabeth held his head in her lap, and her white dress was covered with his blood.

CHAPTER 7
Mike Todd: "He Was My King"

Elizabeth initially noticed Mike Todd while sitting in the MGM commissary. He's quite attractive for a producer, she thought. She recognized him as a fast-talking, smart showman who didn't think it was too much to refer to himself as "Todd Almighty." She remembers seeing images of him with a huge cigar in his mouth in Life magazine. Mike, who was more than two decades Elizabeth's senior, was larger than life and could match her enormous personality. He was born in Minneapolis in 1909, which could be a year or two later than his real birth year. He was the grandson of a Polish rabbi, and his given name was Avrom Hirsch Goldbogen. He was a high school dropout who got his riches in an unconventional way: he operated illicit lottery and bookie establishments and produced burlesque acts.

Her marriage to Wilding had already ended, but she and Mike had become emotionally connected before the divorce was finalized. Elizabeth and Michael Wilding announced their divorce on October 3, 1956. She did not request alimony, simply child support of $250 each month. They would be in each other's lives forever because they shared two children and genuinely cared for each other. Mike called Elizabeth the day after their divorce was made public. He required her presence on the MGM lot. He grabbed her arm and dragged her down a corridor when she arrived. They took an elevator to the next floor and along another hallway, where he directed her to an empty office. They sat across from one other for half an hour as he chatted urgently. See, you're only going to marry one guy, and his name is me!" He told her how much he loved her and how their marriage was unavoidable. Elizabeth had feelings for him, but she thought he was "stark raving mad." He contacted her every night while she was on set filming Raintree County. She admired his strength and the way he compelled people and the world—including her—to conform to his will. He talked her into it, like he did with most things in his life. She began wearing a 29.4-carat emerald-cut diamond, which she referred to as a "friendship ring," while she was still settling the terms of her divorce from Wilding. It was her first significant piece of jewelry, and she referred to it as her "ice skating rink." Elizabeth married Mike in a simple ceremony at Acapulco City Hall on February 2, 1957. Helen Rose designed her third gown, a simple and lovely hydrangea-blue cocktail gown. Eddie Fisher was one of Mike's best men, while Elizabeth's attendants were Debbie Reynolds and Mara (Howard's wife). "I wish for my daughter the same thing that every father wishes—that she will find happiness," her father said in a rare address to the press. "I hope her dreams come true this time."

When Mike and Elizabeth married, they were 47 and 24 years old, respectively. Mike Todd was a completely different person from Michael Wilding, despite the fact that they were separated by more than twenty years. Elizabeth found his vitality alluring, especially after marrying Wilding, a maddeningly prim English gentleman. Mike provided her with the passion and drama she was lacking. When a journalist asked if she loved to fight, she replied without hesitation, "and it always ends up in love-making." Mike was Michael Wilding's remedy. He was macho and sexy, not gentle and nurturing. Debbie Reynolds once witnessed Mike Todd and Elizabeth fighting, which they saw as a precursor to sex. Debbie was shocked.

Mike's Jewishness was not immediately apparent to Sara and Francis. Sara assumed he was Italian and was surprised to learn his given name was Goldbogen. Mike had already produced over twenty musicals, strip shows, and burlesque revues when they met. He'd been bankrupt twice, married twice, and had a son who was two years Elizabeth's senior. Life with Mike was exhilarating. They traveled in magnificent style to promote his famous film Around the

World in 80 Days, flying around the world before flying was widespread. She especially enjoyed coming to Moscow with Mike during the Cold War in 1957 since she could remain unknown there.

Elizabeth had always felt that her new husband was a spy for the United States government. During WWII, he worked as a consultant for the US Army's Special Services section. During the war, the FBI called him and requested tickets to his sold-out event because they had received information that German spies were going that evening. Todd persuaded numerous people to hand over their tickets, which he then turned over to the FBI. Agents nabbed the spy during intermission. He always said he'd tell her why he was going to Moscow in a few years. Mike asked everyone he met, from their drivers to restaurant servers to hotel cleaning staff, what it was like to live in their nation, how the economy was doing, and which politicians they supported. He took long walks with the US ambassador to the Soviet Union, as it was known at the time, because they knew the US embassy was bugged and it was risky to converse inside. Even if it wasn't totally true, Mike wouldn't have minded Elizabeth thinking he was a spy. It suited his larger-than-life demeanor.

She liked feeling cared for, and he liked buying her gifts as much as she did receiving them. He gave her a mink coat, a Renoir, and a diamond tennis bracelet for her 25th birthday. He had two mink coats brought to Elizabeth on their six-month wedding anniversary and asked her which she preferred. "Both!" she exclaimed, delighted. The most spectacular gift was a Cartier jewelry suite: a Burmese ruby-and-diamond necklace, earrings, and bracelet that he gave to his young bride when they were on vacation in August 1957. They were staying at Villa Fiorentina, which is just outside of Monte Carlo. A 20-second home video captures the beautiful enthusiasm of the moment when he hands her the magnificent items. Mike may be seen in the video tenderly putting the necklace around Elizabeth's neck.

During her first trimester of pregnancy with their daughter Liza, she is wearing a strapless bathing suit, her skin bronze and shining. With a joyful grin on her face, she swings her head from side to side to show off the brilliant earrings. Eddie Fisher, Mike's best buddy, is in the pool, squinting up into the sun, watching Elizabeth lavish attention on Mike.

To commemorate the first anniversary of his smash film Around the World in 80 Days, he planned a celebration at Madison Square Garden, the single most showy, attention-grabbing setting for a black-tie party. Eighteen thousand people attended the event, while millions more watched it on television. The film had won five Oscars, including Best Picture, and at the far end of the stadium floor stood a twenty-four-foot Oscar fashioned of gold-colored baby chrysanthemums, with a fourteen-foot-high and thirty-foot-wide cake in the midst. Above the cake was a reproduction of the hot-air balloon from the film. There were thousands of gifts for the audience, including a Cessna plane with flying instruction and six Vespa motorbikes. Elizabeth served as the evening's hostess, dressed in a deep-red velvet gown and the matching Cartier ruby-and-diamond necklace and earrings Mike had given her. And she donned her diamond tiara like a queen (she had always believed Mike was her "king"). Her major responsibility was to cut the cake, which she did with zeal. When they returned home, they chuckled at the mess they'd made.

For the first time, she discussed her wish to retire seriously in October 1956, when she was just twenty-five years old. Her lengthy MGM service would be ended once she finished filming, she reasoned, because Mike had agreed that it would be her final film. They intended to retire to his mansion in Westport, Connecticut, and establish a family there. She was thinking about becoming a Jew. Mike never sat still; there was always something else he needed to do, and Elizabeth was right there with him. She slipped and landed on her tailbone while strolling below deck on a yacht cruise in the Bahamas while pregnant. "I fell six steps and landed on my fat ass," she jokingly explained. The injury aggravated the previous damage to her back. She was in excruciating pain and checked into New York's Columbia-Presbyterian Hospital, where it was discovered that she had shattered three spinal discs. The fetus pushed up under her ribs and put strain on her back, so she was placed in a back brace. Doctors warned her that if she did not get an abortion, she might never walk again, but she refused. She was in an oxygen tent for two weeks and was constantly dizzy. When the physicians decided that the baby had to be delivered, she begged them to wait and let the baby grow, but the situation was too dangerous—both the baby and Elizabeth were in danger.

Elizabeth (Liza) Frances Todd was born via Cesarean section on August 6, 1957, weighing four pounds fourteen ounces. Doctors advised Mike that Elizabeth have a tubal ligation as a form of permanent pregnancy control because giving birth to another child could kill her. Liza was born prematurely and spent the first two months of her life in an oxygen tent. "Mike thought she was a complete miracle. He was persuaded that when he went to see her, shortly after her delivery, when she was in an incubator, clearly in some type of gastric spasm, a small hand came up and made some sort of sign.

Elizabeth's entire world came crashing down on March 22, 1958. She and Mike had been married for thirteen months, had a kid, and had traveled extensively over the world together. Of course, Mike was working on another picture. This time, his vision was Don Quixote, with Elizabeth as Dulcinea, Quixote's idealized wife. Pablo Picasso had already created a film-related drawing. Mike died forty-eight days after they celebrated their first wedding anniversary. He was on his way to New York to be honored as the Friars Club's "Showman of the Year." He flew on his small plane, "The Liz," and was accompanied by his biographer, Art Cohn. Elizabeth was scheduled to accompany him, but she stayed at home because she had a 102-degree fever. Mike entertained Michael and Christopher before departing for his nighttime flight, while Elizabeth sat up in bed watching her little family. Life was as close to wonderful as she had ever experienced.

Elizabeth said that they both experienced a peculiar sensation that night. In their first year of marriage, they had scarcely been apart. "We're overjoyed; I've never been happier in my life." "I'm terrified that something will happen," he whispered as he buried her in kisses. He called her from the airport in Burbank before taking off, saying he would call her from Tulsa, where the jet would need to refuel. He stated that they intended to pick up Jack Benny after a performance in Kansas City and transport him to New York. Elizabeth was unable to sleep. The rain hammered against her window, and the thunder shook the land. When it was 4:00 a.m. and she still hadn't received a call, she attempted to persuade herself that he didn't want to bother her. The children's babysitter arrived at 5:00 a.m. and gave her an alcohol rub to assist decrease her rising temperature. Her mind was racing with terrible ideas. At 6:00 p.m., she dialed her loyal secretary, Dick Hanley. Hanley told her that he was most likely alright, and they hung up. A few minutes later, an AP colleague in Albuquerque called James Bacon. When Bacon answered the phone, his companion exclaimed loudly, "Thank God! That's you!" Bacon's name was on the passenger list of a small plane that had crashed. Bacon phoned Hanley, who had just told Elizabeth that everything was great. Hanley called her doctor, Rex Kennamer, and they went to Elizabeth's residence. It was 8:30 a.m. at the time. They walked together to her room and stood in the doorway, saying nothing. They couldn't think of anything to say. She screamed "No!" repeatedly as she sprinted across the house in her nightgown. Her face was covered with tears, and she plugged her ears, as if refusing to realize the truth would protect her from it. If somebody got too close to her, she shouted. Kennamer eventually got a hold of her and gave her a tranquilizer. Mike's plane had crashed ninety miles west of Albuquerque in the Zuni Mountains. There had been no survivors.

Before Mike died, Elizabeth had been filming Tennessee Williams' masterwork Cat on a Hot Tin Roof for two weeks. When he found out what had happened, the film's director, Richard Brooks, went to see her. She was in her bedroom in "a state of absolute screaming nerves," he added. And she screamed at him. Elizabeth was just 26 years old and lived alone with three tiny children. Liza was just six months old when her father was assassinated. Everyone advised Elizabeth not to attend the funeral, which was scheduled to take place outside of Chicago. They thought she was in too much pain, but she knew she had to go. Debbie Reynolds remained in Los Angeles to care for her children. Howard Hughes provided her with one of his large TWA jets so she wouldn't have to fly commercial and cope with people staring at her. Howard, Dr. Kennamer, Helen Rose, Mike's buddy Eddie Fisher, and Dick Hanley joined her.

On a frigid March day in Zurich, Illinois, 20,000 admirers lined the way to the funeral, with many more waiting inside the Jewish Waldheim Cemetery. Two police cars escorted the six-car funeral procession. People were sipping Coke and having full-fledged picnics at the cemetery, as if it were a carnival. "I recall seeing potato chip bags blowing in the wind." As well as empty Coca-Cola bottles. "And kids crawling over tombstones," Elizabeth explained. The audience was behaving as if it were a movie premiere. Even though she was medicated during the funeral, she felt violated. Elizabeth got out of the car and put a black glove over her face. Dr. Kennamer, her twenty-eight-year-old stepson Michael Todd Jr., and Howard physically supported her. Elizabeth, like Jackie Kennedy, was gorgeous even in her sadness after her husband died suddenly five years later. She was dressed to the nines, with hanging diamond earrings, a hat with a veil, and a black mink on her arm. People lunged at her as she walked from the automobile to her husband's casket, which was surrounded by a rose-covered carpet. People would sometimes reach out to touch her in order to prove to themselves that she was genuine. Mike, she added, had made her feel whole, and now he was gone. She put Mike's pajamas under her pillow at home in Los Angeles and requested the housekeepers not to change the sheets. She wanted the scent of him to linger as long as possible.

She became an insomniac and began taking sleeping pills after the shock of Mike's death and years of feeling used by her parents, a habit she was never able to break. Later in life, her friend George Hamilton described her as having "psychoscopic pain." She was experiencing every young mother's worst fear. She went down the circular staircase a week after Mike died and discovered her son Michael Wilding Jr. in the living room, staring out the window and screaming in a monotone voice, "Mike is dead! Mike is no longer alive! Mike is no longer alive!" It was like something out of a horror film. Worse, nineteen years after the plane disaster, criminals dug up Mike's body in the Jewish Waldheim Cemetery. They were seeking for a diamond ring that was said to be buried with him. All they discovered were remnants of charred clothing, ash, and fragments of a seat belt, reliving Elizabeth's horror and terror at his death. But there was so much to recall in terms of beauty and romanticism. Elizabeth brought out the Cartier ruby-and-diamond suite Mike had given her and set it on her bed to enjoy in the sunlight from time to time.

CHAPTER 8
Eddie Fisher: "He Kept Mike Todd Alive"

Mike Todd stood for safety and untainted love and protection. And it had all vanished in an instant. Elizabeth would have to search within herself for what he represented, but she was only twenty-six years old and not yet strong enough. She was now on her own, with three children to raise. Mike's financial situation had always been precarious, and his life insurance did not cover his death because of a condition that barred payout if he died in a small-plane crash. Looking back, it is evident that Elizabeth was suffering from post-traumatic stress disorder. She couldn't eat, and she dropped eight pounds in the three weeks following Mike's death. She couldn't watch television, read, or concentrate for long periods of time. The medical examiner had to use dental records to identify the bodies aboard the plane, and the only piece of Mike's that survived the crash was his wedding band, which had become twisted in the fire. She went to her brother's house in La Jolla and spent some time with his family. She took long walks on the beach and slept in a sleeping bag for fourteen or fifteen hours a night in a much more basic home than she was used to.

The studio only gave Elizabeth two weeks to recover—an insufficient amount of time—but having that project to complete gave her a sense of purpose, and she said it had saved her in some ways. She was only at ease when she was Maggie, the film's attractive, calculating, and sexually unsatisfied character. But she needed to return to work not just for the money, but also for her mental health. Richard Brooks claimed that her suffering had permanently altered her. The players are scated at a huge table covered with food in the scenario. Normally, the food would have been sitting for hours, doused in fly spray to protect it. However, Ives and Brooks planned to have fresh ham, sourdough bread, and veggies available for each take so that Elizabeth would be compelled to eat actual food rather than pretending. For the first time in days, she ate hungrily, and she never forgot this simple act of kindness. Elizabeth penned a note to Brooks on April 18, 1958, less than a month after Todd's death, and crossed out "Mrs. Michael Todd," which was written in fine handwriting on her stationery. That was no longer her identity.

Any moments involving Big Daddy's impending demise were very difficult to film. "Nothing's ever the way you plan, is it?" remarked Judith Anderson, who played Big Daddy's patient wife, in one scene. Elizabeth was on the verge of losing it, but she persisted. Her performance as a sexually starved lady attempting to speak with her alcoholic, traumatized, and closeted gay husband, who lives in the past and refuses to interact with her, was electric. The picture was a tremendous success when it was released in 1958. Elizabeth was adrift. Eddie Fisher was so popular at the time that Queen Elizabeth II and President Eisenhower were fans. He enjoyed being followed by swarms of young ladies, making a lot of money (he earned $7,500 per week as the main act at New York's Paramount Theatre), going out late, and gambling. He looked up to celebrities like Frank Sinatra and Mike Todd, who led extravagant lives. Mike referred to Fisher as "my boy." Fisher adored Mike so much that when he and Debbie had their baby three weeks before the plane tragedy, he named him Mike. Elizabeth and Fisher were the two individuals in the world who loved Mike the most, and they grieved together. Elizabeth accompanied Debbie and Fisher to the Tropicana's June debut of his play. Her first public appearance since her husband's funeral. Elizabeth called Fisher on his thirty-first birthday in August to inform him she had a gift for him. It was the engraved money clip she'd given Mike with a quote she and Fisher had heard Mike say hundreds of times: "Poverty is a state of mind." I've been broke several times, but never impoverished."

She flew to New York two weeks later, when Fisher was filming his Coca-Cola television show. He was exactly what she needed to remind her of Mike. They made little attempt to conceal their romance. They spent Labor Day weekend at Grossinger's, a Catskills resort where he began his career and also where he and Debbie married in 1955. When they returned to Manhattan, they dined at the stylish Quo Vadis and danced at the popular Blue Angel nightclub. Carrie, Debbie and Fisher's daughter, became acquainted with Elizabeth later in life and questioned her if she had ever loved her father. Elizabeth responded, "He kept Mike Todd alive." Debbie, on the other hand, publicly laid the responsibility completely at Elizabeth's feet. MGM carefully developed and pushed a picture of Debbie with diaper pins stuck to her top. Debbie summoned a press conference, which was broadcast live on television stations around the country. "Elizabeth has stolen my husband," she said, her eyes welling up. What better way to sell the blue-eyed strawberry-blonde than as a woman scorned? Debbie increased her earnings from $125,000 to $250,000.

The truth was that their marriage had been in danger nearly from the start, and they had sought aid from a marriage counselor who had been unable to assist them. Elizabeth thought to herself, "Somebody needs me, maybe I can make somebody happy." Six months after Mike's death, she took the unwise move of speaking with powerful gossip columnist Hedda Hopper. Hopper had been Elizabeth's acquaintance since Sara cozied up to her when Elizabeth was a child star. Hopper saw herself as Hollywood's moral arbiter; Elizabeth had been an actor for eighteen years and felt she needed to do something to soothe the public outrage. She informed Hopper that the Fishers' marriage had ended. Later, in her Beverly Hills Hotel bungalow, Hopper begged Elizabeth for forgiveness. "Forgive yourself," Elizabeth replied. She realized at that point that no one in the media was her buddy. The press was continually circling like vultures. A reporter once asked Elizabeth, "How does it feel to have your life so well documented?" "Not documented," she said, "dominated... you have to always be on your best behavior." Hopper taught Elizabeth a vital lesson: "The public puts you up on that pedestal, then they wait like vultures to tear you down."

She was nominated for an Academy Award in 1959 for her performance as Maggie the Cat in Cat on a Hot Tin Roof. It was her second nomination; she had previously been nominated for Raintree County in 1958. But she was afraid she wouldn't win since she was a "bad girl." She was accurate; she was defeated by Susan Hayward's I Want to Live! The Theater Owners of America punished her by scrapping her nomination for "Star of the Year" and issuing a nasty statement. "The movie industry is at the mercy of public opinion," it said, "and bestowing the honor on Miss Taylor at this time was out of the question." Elizabeth, who thrived in her femininity and sexuality and could not stand deception, would not submit to such censorship. Elizabeth's cleavage seemed to get a lot of attention, and during one wardrobe test, a man whose job title was really B.I., short for "Bust Inspector," took one look at her in her low-cut outfit and instantly requested for a stepladder.

She and Lerner, who was in his late fifties at the time, had an affair that lasted until 1961. They met in London pubs and hotel rooms, where she told Lerner that things between her and Fisher were already deteriorating. "I thought I could keep Mike's memory alive in that way, but I only have his ghost." She spent the rest of her life hunting for males who shared some characteristics with Mike. Lerner was a Yale University graduate and a Brandeis University professor of American Civilization; she referred to him as her "intellectual Mike Todd." She enjoyed sex and knew she could get practically any man she desired. And she made no apologies about occupying space in a man's world. Lerner speculated that she might be egotistical. She snapped at him when he said he couldn't wait to present her to the dignitaries and heads of state he wanted to invite to their house for dinner parties after they were married. "Fuck you!" she exclaimed. "I see these folks without you now. I'm the one who attracts them. I don't need you to bring them to me."

When Fisher found out about her relationship with Lerner he was furious. Even though she knew that Fisher would never be what she needed, she did not want him to abandon her. She had been traumatized by Mike's death, and she clung to him for a sense of security. And she thought that her three small children needed a father figure in their lives, so when Debbie eventually agreed to a divorce, Elizabeth pushed to get married as quickly as possible. She also thought that their story would be much less intriguing to the press once they were married. And Elizabeth was finally free to make a big professional decision. She was offered the lead in the film version of Tennessee Williams's Suddenly, Last Summer. Gore Vidal adapted the macabre gothic play with themes of homosexuality, incest, and cannibalism for the screen. Her business advisers told her not to do it, but she loved the controversial script and considered her character, Catherine Holly, an irresistible challenge. Holly is a traumatized woman who fights back against doctors who declare her mentally ill as a way to silence her.

Suddenly, Last Summer began filming in May 1959. Elizabeth would be reunited with her beloved Monty for the film, and she would get to act with Katharine Hepburn, whom she had idolized and who had once frostily signed her autograph book at MGM. Hepburn played Mrs. Venable, an eccentric and incredibly rich older woman who volunteers to give money to a struggling state-run asylum if the doctor, played by Monty, will agree to lobotomize her niece, Catherine, played by Elizabeth. On March 3, 1959, a year after Mike's death, Elizabeth officially converted to Judaism at Temple Israel in Hollywood. It was a way to keep him close and to find meaning during her grief. Raised as a Christian Scientist, she felt a deep connection to the Jewish faith and its people, especially having seen how they were persecuted during World War II. Her Hebrew name was Elisheba (the Hebrew word for "Elizabeth") Rachel (who was the favorite wife of Jacob). When Mike was killed, a rabbi named Dr. Max Nussbaum of Temple Israel came to visit Elizabeth. She kept asking him why Mike died, and Nussbaum told her that he did not have an answer. As the pain got less excruciating, she wanted to find out the answer herself, and she went back to see Nussbaum again.

Taylor and Fisher married on May 12, 1959, fourteen months after Mike Todd's death, in Temple Beth Sholom in Las Vegas. Elizabeth donned a belted green cocktail dress by Jean Louis rather than her usual Helen Rose, with a diaphanous cloak thrown beautifully around her head. Her three children's stepfather had changed. Michael Wilding Jr. was six, Christopher Wilding was four, and Liza Todd was just two years old. Because everything was now out in the open, their marriage did serve to dampen some of the press coverage, as she had intended. Nonetheless, some colonists were outraged, with the majority directing their rage at the bride rather than the groom.

CHAPTER 9
Trailblazer

According to producer Walter Wanger, Elizabeth was a modern-day Cleopatra who got what she wanted and never apologized for it. He had asked Elizabeth about the role when she was married to Mike Todd, but she refused since she didn't want to be apart from Mike. Wanger ran into Elizabeth at the Polo Lounge, the legendary restaurant in the Beverly Hills Hotel that was formerly known as "Hollywood's commissary," after Mike's death, and handed her a copy of The Life and Times of Cleopatra. She despised the script when she first read it, but she wanted to play the woman who conquered civilizations. She believed it was the most amazing role ever created for a woman. During the filming of BUtterfield 8, 20th Century Fox commissioned research on ancient Egypt and Rome. After two years, employees had completed fifteen thick, bound, and indexed volumes. Cleopatra would very definitely bankrupt one of the world's largest studios, and it would alter Elizabeth's life in unanticipated ways.

To put her audacious demand in context, Natalie Wood, a fellow star who fought her own battles with studio executives and received three Oscar nominations by the age of twenty-five, was paid $250,000 ($2.4 million in today's dollars) for her role in the blockbuster 1961 film adaptation of the Broadway musical West Side Story. Elizabeth demanded four times what Wood was earning. Breakfast at Tiffany's earned Audrey Hepburn $750,000 ($7.2 million now). But Elizabeth took advantage of the opportunity and demanded more. She understood her worth and was never hesitant to ask for what she desired—or to walk away if her demands were not granted. But Fox refused to give up. She was enjoying a bubble bath in their sumptuous Dorchester apartment in London when the phone rang. Fisher answered the phone, knocked on the bathroom door, and informed Elizabeth that it was the studio—yet again. Elizabeth reiterated her demand: $1 million and 10% of the total profit. Fisher conveyed the news, and Elizabeth heard another banging on the door a minute later: they had finally caved. She burst out laughing and dived into the water.

She was to be paid $125,000 for sixteen weeks of work, followed by $50,000 per week; $3,000 per week for living expenses, and 10% of the absolute total. The film would be shot in Todd-AO, Mike Todd's high-resolution widescreen film format, and first-class round-trip airfare would be supplied for her retinue, which included her three children. During filming, she and Fisher stayed at the Dorchester Hotel like members of the royal family. When she insisted on having Sydney Guilaroff do her hair again, the British labor union erupted, so it was determined that he would do her hair in the early mornings but not on the Pinewood set, where only British stylists were employed. Elizabeth was given forty outfits and headdresses to wear. Fisher was also given a job; he was paid $1,500 a week ($14,500 in today's dollars) to make sure Elizabeth showed up for work. And she eventually requested that her close friend Roddy McDowall play the calculating Octavian in the film. Mark Antony was played by Stephen Boyd, and Caesar was played by Peter Finch.

Cleopatra ultimately cost $44 million to produce (about $425 million in today's currencies), with the star's opulent lifestyle, including chauffeurs and villas, adding to the cost. But Elizabeth realized that without her, the studio would be nothing. The massive set was constructed on nine acres at Pinewood Studios outside of London. They possessed enough building materials to construct at least 40 houses, including 300 gallons of paint, 142 miles of tubular steel, 20,000 cubic feet of wood, and 7 tons of nails. Cleopatra's white marble palace interior was twice as tall as Grand Central Terminal. Temples, ponds, and pools were featured in the $600,000 set. When the London fog crept in, seven hundred extras got lost in the nine acres of ancient Alexandria. The truth was that London's foul weather was doing havoc on Elizabeth's fragile health. On September 30, 1960, for example, Wanger observed that the temperature was just 45 degrees and that there was only two minutes and twenty seconds of sunshine. Elizabeth had called in sick that day with a scratchy throat. Skouras chastised Wanger for insisting on Elizabeth as the film's star. Elizabeth believed the script was still not working after two major modifications. She was an acute critic since she had been reading scripts since she was nine years old, and she could tell very quickly when a script worked and when it didn't.

Elizabeth became severely ill after Capote left, with a fever that lingered above 103 degrees and refused to break. Her private nurse was so concerned about her heavy breathing and blue-tinged nails that she called the Dorchester's front desk to request a doctor on March 4, 1961. Fortunately, a party was going on down the hall from Elizabeth's suite, and one of London's top anesthesiologists was present. When he examined Elizabeth, he found that the congestion in her lungs was causing her to suffocate. She was diagnosed with acute pneumonia in the hospital. She was placed in an iron lung-like automated respirator. She went in and out of consciousness during her hospitalization. Outside the hospital, fans and reporters gathered. Flowers and gifts were delivered from all over the world. Elizabeth's death was even reported at one point.

When Elizabeth was nearing the end of her life, the studio contacted Joan Collins, who was already under contract with Fox and was previously being considered for the role when the film was to be done on a much smaller scale, if she would be available to come to London. They warned Elizabeth that she might not make it. "I was appalled," Collins said. "I asked, 'How could they have thought of doing such a thing?'" Elizabeth is a friend of mine, not a close friend, but a friend, and I couldn't possibly ignore her.' That's equivalent to walking on someone's grave." Wanger needed to reassure Skouras and everyone else that Elizabeth was still alive and well. Fourteen days after her illness began, her lungs began to clear and color began to return to her face. In the capacity of manager/husband, Eddie Fisher declared, "Elizabeth is not going to do Cleopatra in England." She thrives on sunlight and requires it. That means no more work in England, New York, or anywhere else with severe weather."

She was 29 years old, yet she felt like she had just gotten out of the womb. She knew she needed to change her personal life, but she also wanted to reconsider her work life. Capote, who had just seen Elizabeth and her "busboy," was relieved when Elizabeth was well enough for him to go to the hospital and see her. She was practically out of breath as she described every horrible detail to him. "A kind of thick black fire filled my chest and lungs." To drain the flames, they had to cut a hole in my throat. When she finally left the facility at the end of March, she traveled home to Los Angeles, where her Rolls-Royce was greeted by a crowd. People smiled and waved this time instead of spitting at her, as they had when she first arrived in London. Elizabeth made her first public speech since her sickness on March 24, 1961, saying, "I didn't know there was so much love in the world." On April 17, 1961, as she arrived at the Santa Monica Civic Forum for the 33rd Academy Awards, 2,500 people sat on bleacher seats trying to catch a sight of her. Her least favorite film, BUtterfield 8, had gotten her an Oscar nomination. She wore Dior couture with a mink capelet, white gloves, and long diamond earrings, accented by a tan she got from a quick trip to Palm Springs with Fisher after they returned from London.

CHAPTER 10
Le Scandale

A teenage Elizabeth relaxed languidly by the pool at actor Stewart Granger's beautiful Los Angeles estate in the 1950s, looking stunning in a bikini and reading a book. She was used to socializing with superstars and their hairdressers, publicists, screenwriters, and studio executives at industry parties. The visitors were sipping Bloody Marys and highballs on a Sunday morning. On the rocks, Richard Burton was sipping a Scotch. Elizabeth closed her book and pushed her sunglasses to the tip of her nose as she heard his booming voice from across the pool. He could feel her staring at him and thought she was looking right through him. He smiled, and after a few seconds, she returned his feeble smile. She sipped her drink and went back to her reading. This was the first time the most famous Hollywood couple of the twentieth century had ever met, and things were not looking good. Richard Burton was born Richard Jenkins Jr. in Pontrhydyfen, South Wales, on November 10, 1925. He was the twelfth of thirteen children born into a mining family in Wales. Elizabeth admired the fact that, unlike Mike Todd and Nicky Hilton, he obtained scholarships based on his intellect rather than his family's wealth.

Richard attended Oxford on a scholarship for a year and served in the Royal Air Force from 1945 to 1947. He married Sybil Williams, a fellow Welsh actor who had acted in one of his early films, in 1949. Kate and Jessica were their two daughters. He worked in the theaters of London and New York and was influenced by his friend Sir John Gielgud. Richard returned to London at the famed Old Vic Theatre in 1954, earning $140 per week and appearing in Hamlet, The Tempest, and King John. He went through a period of professional despair before being offered the role of King Arthur in Camelot on Broadway, for which he received critical acclaim. Winston Churchill even chose Richard to be the narrator of The Valiant Years, a television documentary based on his memoirs. Richard was once again noticed by Hollywood, and he was offered the role of Mark Antony in Cleopatra.

Cleopatra began filming again in Rome in September 1961. Monday through Saturday, filming took place six days a week. Elizabeth, who was still delicate after her near-death experience, was pampered like a queen while they were filming. Her screenplay was encased in Moroccan leather, and her chair was fashioned of California redwood and Russian leather, a present from Mankiewicz. Taylor and Fisher moved into their spacious home in a quiet park on Via Appia on September 1, 1961. It was a few minutes from the set and cost the studio an absurd three thousand dollars a month at the time. Michael Junior, Christopher, Liza, their nanny, an assistant, and seven animals: a St. Bernard, a collie, three terriers, and two Siamese cats accompanied Elizabeth.

Elizabeth spent at least two hours at work doing her own cosmetics, including her extensive and overdone catlike eye makeup. She adorned her lids with spangles, eyeshadow, and heavy black eyeliner. It was a fanciful portrayal of a gorgeous queen in perfect command of her sensuality. When she wasn't working, Elizabeth was planning to adopt a fourth kid. She desired at least six children, but she was unable to have another kid because she had given birth three times via Cesarean section and had a tubal ligation. She and Fisher intended to adopt, and because celebrities without stable homes were not considered good candidates, her agent, Kurt Frings, asked his Austrian client, Maria Schell, if she could inquire into adoptions in Germany. Schell discovered six babies in need of homes. Elizabeth arrived at Schell's house and discovered an eight-month-old baby girl in a wicker laundry basket. Maria was named after Maria Schell. Baby Maria underwent one major operation to repair her hip, and she spent five years in various body casts. Her fourth marriage was falling apart at the time of the adoption. Fisher saw his role as her guardian, manager, and minder, which was not particularly romantic.

When Elizabeth first saw Richard on set, he approached her and remarked, "Has anybody ever told you that you're a very pretty girl?" She was not impressed in the least. "Here's the great lover, wit, and intellectual of Wales, and he comes out with a line like that." She was aware of Richard's notoriety. ("Richard, you'd screw a snake, wouldn't you?" Joan Collins told him once. "Only if it was wearing a skirt, darling," he said.) Elizabeth didn't want to be just another notch on his sleeve. However, on January 22, 1962, Elizabeth and Richard shot their first scene together. Richard had gone on a drinking binge the night before, consuming all he could get his hands on, including beverages left behind at the bar. He hadn't slept in two nights, and it was five o'clock in the afternoon. He went to get a cup of coffee, but he couldn't put it to his lips since his hands were trembling so severely. He requested Elizabeth's assistance. He has the same compelling personality as Mike Todd and the same brilliance as Max Lerner. She was smitten the moment she saw him. "I get an orgasm just listening to that voice of his," she said.

Walter Wanger, the producer, stood on the set, amused, as the two of them huddled together discussing during their first days of filming. Elizabeth was dressed in a yellow silk gown, while Richard was dressed in a knee-length Roman toga. When it was time to start filming, they parted ways and went their separate ways, yet an invisible rope always seemed to pull them back together. Richard and Sybil and Eddie and Elizabeth went out with another couple one evening, and Fisher kept telling them they should call it a night. Even though it was just 9:30 p.m., Elizabeth was relieved to be out, seated across the table from Richard. Richard, who was always the center of attention at a party, kept chatting, and he kept refilling his wine and discreetly passing it to Elizabeth, so she had many drinks without Fisher noticing. Truman Capote sympathized with Fisher. "He was madly in love with her, and she was incredibly rude to him." Richard was among the attendees during a dinner party she hosted at their villa. Fisher stood up and went over to the piano to sing a tune while telling everyone a story.

Richard was a respected stage actor before, but once he was linked with Elizabeth he became world famous, and he was enjoying it. Their affair ushered in an era of decadence and glamor never seen before. He bought her gifts at Bulgari's store on the elegant Via Condotti and presented them to her, even while Sybil was visiting him in Rome. When filming moved to the shores of the Mediterranean, Richard marveled at Elizabeth's sense of humor. She would climb a ladder from her yacht to Cleopatra's barge, where Cleopatra is planning world domination, and she would wear her heavy costume over her bikini. In between takes, she would take off the costume and sunbathe on the deck of the yacht in her full Cleopatra eye makeup.

Their tumultuous relationship fueled their roles as the scandalous Mark Antony and Cleopatra. When Richard flaunted a blond showgirl in front of Elizabeth, she shot him an icy glance on camera, prompting Richard to take her aside and say, "Don't get my Welsh temper up." On March 8, 1962, a newspaper said that Richard would never leave Sybil. Richard and Elizabeth were back on by late March. They went out to dinner on Rome's prestigious Via Veneto and stayed until three o'clock in the morning. They were, nevertheless, madly in love with one other. One particularly heated letter is in an envelope addressed to Elizabeth and labeled "Very Private and Personal." "Read my diary," Richard once wrote to her. There's a little bit about you in it, and I thought you'd like to know what it's like to fuck you." Photographs of them kissing on yachts in the Mediterranean and dancing at nightclubs on Rome's Via Veneto not only pushed the Cold War to the back pages, but rumors about their romance also pushed John Glenn's orbit of the Earth out of the spotlight in 1962. No other celebrity couple had ever received as much attention. Jack Brodsky, Fox's head of American press, couldn't walk into a café in Rome without being besieged by paparazzi attempting to bribe him for photos of Richard and Elizabeth on location.

Their affair was such enormous news that even the Vatican was paying attention. In an April 1962 open letter in Vatican City's weekly newspaper Elizabeth was charged with "erotic vagrancy" because she was sleeping with Burton while still married to Fisher. The Vatican talked of "this insult to the nobility of the hearth." Elizabeth was kick-starting the sexual revolution of the late 1960s and '70s in the United States that would drastically shift the cultural landscape and would expand the agency that women had over their own bodies. A 1964 5,000-word bylined cover essay in Time magazine questioned the changing morality of the era, "in which pleasure is increasingly considered an almost constitutional right rather than a privilege, in which self-denial is increasingly seen as foolishness rather than virtue. While science has reduced fear of long-dreaded earthly dangers, such as pregnancy and VD, skepticism has diminished fear of divine punishment.

During the 1950s, there was "good" and "bad" behavior, and the kind of moral certitude that Elizabeth found repellent. She never lived her life in black and white; to her there were always many shades of gray and reasons why people make the decisions they make. But this massive shift took time. The FDA did not approve the birth control pill until 1960, and it was not until 1965 that Planned Parenthood of Connecticut won the U.S. Supreme Court case Griswold v. Connecticut, which rolled back state and local laws outlawing the use of contraception, even by married couples. The problem for Elizabeth was that she was just a little too early. When her passionate affair with Richard riveted the world, many women did not yet have access to the pill (it was not until a 1972 Supreme

Court case that birth control became legal for all women, married and single), and the morals of the 1950s were still very much intact. In 1962, after the Vatican had denounced her, Elizabeth was to shoot Cleopatra's grand entrance into Rome. She was terrified, because she assumed the six thousand Italian extras hated her. They were likely Catholic, after all.

Elizabeth's role in the film quagmire was over after more than 200 days of filming. She was unable to follow Richard to Egypt for the final two weeks of filming due to her public conversion to Judaism and support for Israel. Elizabeth retreated to Chalet Ariel, the remote property she and Fisher purchased in Switzerland, which would serve as both her sanctuary and her sole real home for years. Six months of "Le Scandale " had devoured Elizabeth, both by her love for Richard and by the knowledge of how many people they had harmed. Eddie Fisher was unimportant to her since she saw herself as more of a parental figure than his lover at the time. However, Sybil and Richard's girls were weighing heavily on Elizabeth's mind. She filed for divorce from Fisher. She grew to despise him, and she couldn't shake the image of him holding a gun to her head one night in Villa Papa. Fisher had removed the bedroom door knobs and was caressing her head with a rifle as they lay in bed together. That was the dreadful night he told her she was "too pretty" to kill. She always maintained in touch with her ex-boyfriends, "except Edna," she claimed many times over the years, referring to Fisher by her nickname.

When 20th Century Fox was nearly bankrupt due to Cleopatra, Monroe was fired from her final film, Something's Gotta Give, which was never completed. Monroe believed Fox fired her because they were overspending on Elizabeth and her over budget epic. Monroe was paid $100,000, as opposed to Elizabeth's $1 million for Cleopatra. Elizabeth informed a friend twenty years later that she had called Monroe and offered to leave Cleopatra and only return if

Monroe was rehired. Marilyn was moved by the offer, but she felt that such a public act of rebellion against the studio would only harm them both. Elizabeth got it. She had been in the industry for a much longer time and had seen it all.

During the summer of 1962, Elizabeth and Richard were separated for two months. Her parents were staying nearby, while Richard lived in Céligny, a small Swiss village near Geneva, about a two-hour drive away. Richard called one day and invited her to dine at Chateau de Chillon on Lake Geneva at two o'clock. They were approaching from opposing directions, and she was riding in the backseat with her parents. They hadn't seen one other since Cleopatra was wrapped, and now he was there, green eyes gleaming against a deep tan. She missed Richard so badly that she resolved to be there for him whenever he needed her. She would be satisfied with life as his mistress because it was better than nothing. They were stuck in this awkward dance for fifteen months while Richard contemplated leaving Sybil. Elizabeth's children were traumatized by this moment in their mother's life. Michael and Christopher didn't see their father very often, Liza's father had died, and Maria had never seen Eddie Fisher. Richard adopted Maria after he and Elizabeth married in 1964, and she is the couple's soul child. Maria recalls sitting across from Eddie Fisher at a dinner party in New York in the early 1990s. She hadn't seen him since his divorce from Elizabeth. With tears in his eyes, he remarked to Maria, "You were meant to be one of my children." She didn't know what to say at such a difficult time. She finally felt like she could stop looking when she was with Richard. "What do you think will become of us?" she wondered to her friend Truman Capote. I believe when you find what you've always desired, that's when the end begins, not the beginning."

CHAPTER 11
Crazy, Stupid Love, 1964–1973

Following the completion of Cleopatra, Elizabeth and Richard were in London filming The VIPs, a film that Elizabeth knew was not going to be a cinematic masterpiece; it was merely a means for her to be with Richard. That was all she cared about, as was he. Richard had been requested to read the script for the film, which is about a bunch of jetsetters who are stranded at Heathrow Airport after their plane is grounded. Richard didn't like the script, but Elizabeth could tell it was going to make them a lot of money. While filming The VIPs, Elizabeth and Richard resided in separate suites at the Dorchester in London. Elizabeth had been separated from Fisher, but Richard was still living a double life and paying visits to Sybil at their London house. He had to make a decision. "I love my first wife, Sybil, but in a different way," Richard explained. Sybil and their daughters moved to New York in April 1963. She filed for divorce citing "abandonment and cruel and inhuman treatment," as well as the fact that her spouse was "constantly in the company of another woman." They separated in December, and Sybil was awarded custody and a $1 million settlement. Richard's remorse at abandoning Sybil and his girls was unbreakable, especially given how much time he spent with Elizabeth's children, including her daughter Liza, Kate's age. His diary entries demonstrate his admiration for Liza's tenacity and brilliance. "Understand that I love both children [Kate and Liza] to the point of idolatry," he wrote in 1969. In the back of his mind, he felt like a phony who had abandoned Wales and his working-class coal-mining family in exchange for a Faustian deal with Elizabeth to seek a wealthy career in Hollywood over his dream of becoming a respected writer. All of this exacerbated Richard's drinking, and it became clear that he had an unsolvable issue. He couldn't stop once he started. Chris recalls how difficult it was to be the kid of the world's most famous actress, particularly during her early years with Richard, when the children lived in a separate apartment on a different level at the Dorchester. They also spent a lot of time at boarding school, where they were looked after by Norma Heyman and Liz Smith (not the columnist, whom Elizabeth also knew) and nannies.

The initial Cleopatra advertisements featured Elizabeth and Richard in costume but did not disclose the film's title or even their names. They were the first prominent famous couple whose identity or explanation was unnecessary. The VIPs were treated similarly. The two were depicted on movie posters with the phrase "She and He..." People were voyeuristic about seeing Elizabeth and Richard act together because they wanted to see if their sexual attraction would be obvious on the TV. On June 12, 1963, ten thousand spectators packed the Rivoli Theatre in New York City for the premiere of Cleopatra, a record audience for a New York debut. And Elizabeth was not even present. The reception was mixed. According to the Herald Tribune, "the mountain of notoriety has produced a mouse." The New York Times dubbed it "one of the great epic films of our day."

Elizabeth understood what it took to make a successful film, and she expected the backlash when she read the script in 1959. She wanted Cleopatra's intentions to be more evident; she was aware of the difficulty in depicting the world's most renowned female queen as a savvy politician and a lady controlled by love. Elizabeth had negotiated such an unprecedented deal for herself that when she complained that Fox was receiving an unfair share of the initial gross, the studio responded: "Miss Taylor failed to appear for work on at least forty working days in Italy, which cost the company between $150,000 and $175,000 per day." Elizabeth sued Fox for the agreed-upon cut, and Fox sued both her and Richard for a total of $50 million: $20 million against Elizabeth for her absences and for exposing herself to "scorn, ridicule, and unfavorable publicity as a result of her conduct and deportment, during and after production, and while the film was being distributed, so as to become offensive to good taste and morals and to depreciate the commercial value of the film." According to Fox, Richard was guilty of the same conduct, but they only sued him for $5 million. The remaining $25 million was essentially punishment for their affair. Never mind that Darryl Zanuck, the studio's head, was notorious for abusing his authority and forcing young women to sleep with him in exchange for stardom. The claim eventually died in a series of out-of-court settlements, but Elizabeth was haunted by it for years.

She handled the torrent of unfavorable reviews and lawsuits with grace. When The VIPs came out in September 1963, the reviews were nearly as harsh. The problem was her million-dollar fee. Because "Le Scandale" had made them notoriously wealthy and powerful, the public had expected more from Richard and Elizabeth. Elizabeth's personal life was coming into focus as her professional life unraveled. Richard and Sybil were officially divorced by April 1963, while Elizabeth's divorce from Fisher was finalized in March 1964. It took so long because Fisher demanded more of Cleopatra's revenue, and at one point even demanded $1 million in exchange for agreeing to a divorce. He dragged the process out by later claiming that their divorce was illegitimate. He went to the press and accused Elizabeth of bigamy, to which she responded, "He's got to be joking." On March 15, 1964, Elizabeth and Richard married in Montreal. She was 32, and Richard was 38; he was her fifth husband, and she became his second wife. Because a traveling commercial would have aroused the paparazzi, they went aboard a chartered plane from Toronto, where Richard was doing Hamlet, to Montreal. She and Richard disliked crowds and were afraid that someone would hurt them; Richard was particularly terrified that someone would throw acid in their faces. Elizabeth had recurring dreams of being caught in a crowd and being shot with a gun. When they arrived in Boston for Richard's performance in Hamlet at the

Sheraton-Plaza Hotel, three thousand people crammed into the lobby and spilled out onto the street. They were absolutely surrounded.

They were on the Manson family's list of celebrity targets in the late 1960s, with Steve McQueen and Frank Sinatra. Susan Atkins, who confessed to killing Sharon Tate, stated that she intended to use a heated knife to gouge out Elizabeth's trademark blue eyes and castrate Richard Burton. Elizabeth and Richard recruited professional security guards to protect their children, who were attending various boarding schools across Europe. They looked for their mother's whereabouts in the newspaper. According to FBI archives, Elizabeth became involved in a conspiracy to extort money from numerous other prominent women in 1978, including Jackie Onassis, the only woman alive with the same level of renown (apart from Queen Elizabeth II). Onassis had received a letter demanding that she inform Farrah Fawcett, Elizabeth Taylor, and Cornelia Wallace, who was married to Alabama governor George Wallace, that they needed to send $25,000 or they would all be killed. Being a public figure was nothing new to Elizabeth, but the attention she received with Richard was unlike anything she had ever experienced. During that frantic period, Roddy McDowall captured some of the most candid images of Elizabeth. One depicts a crowd encircling the Burtons following a Hamlet performance. McDowall informed Elizabeth that he planned to photograph the scene from the top of the building next door.

They discovered the tranquil coastal village of Puerto Vallarta in Mexico. When Elizabeth was still legally married to Fisher, she lived in Casa Kimberly, a Mediterranean-style villa on a hillside overlooking the Pacific Ocean across the street from a casita where Richard remained. They had a bridge built to connect the two homes, resulting in a beautiful compound. The bridge was created as a duplicate of Venice's Bridge of Sighs, and it provided them with the solitude they needed to go between the two residences without drawing attention to themselves. They kept the windows of Casa Kimberly open in their refuge, reveling in their relative anonymity. They went to Mexico whenever they could. The money and power were appealing to Richard, but the lack of solitude and Elizabeth's expensive way of life were wearing on him—he began referring to their combined reputation as "diabolical." Their brawls were so legendary that when they stayed in hotels, admirers would try to get rooms below theirs and stand on chairs with their glasses to their ears to hear them yell at each other.

Even after several years together, they still had feelings for each other. "I still get a thrill now and then, as I did this afternoon in the dining room, because Richard went upstairs to get something and I really broke out in sort of goose bumps and shivered slightly when I saw him walking across the dining room toward me because—I love to look at him." Every now and again, he looks so bloody attractive and desirable that I wonder how I would feel if he wasn't my husband and I just happened to see him passing through my dining room—would he have the same effect on me?" She had a fantasy that when they were in their late forties, they would retire and have one primary residence, putting a stop to their hectic lifestyle. Richard would become a writer (he had too much talent), and she would leave acting to take care of their home and entertain their friends.

But, throughout the 1960s and early 1970s, Elizabeth was still on magazine covers, this time with Richard. They discovered something in each other that they couldn't find elsewhere. Elizabeth stated in a 1969 love letter to Richard, "As long as he loves her, everything is O.K. pimples, stupid hips, double chins, and all—She loved him more than her life and always will.—Wife." Their relationship was inherently flawed, yet it is evident that Elizabeth and Richard adored each other and helped each other improve as actors. Richard was displeased with their first scene in Cleopatra. Elizabeth's facial expressions appeared too subtly controlled, as did her emotions. But when he saw her on-screen, he realized she was doing a lot more than he could see while he was standing next to her.

Decades later, the director of a television movie Elizabeth acted in in the mid-1980s, Arthur Allen Seidelman, remembers how talented she was as an actress. Her character had to be standing next to a table in a specific position. "She knew exactly how to get herself there, and it was completely natural," he explained. "There are times when you need to direct and times when you just need to get out of the way." And you went out of the way with Elizabeth." Philip Burton, the man Richard looked up to as a mentor and father figure and whose name he took, was a member of the faculty at the American Musical and Dramatic Academy. He asked Richard and Elizabeth if they would perform a poetry reading to benefit the school. He was taken aback when they both answered yes. Elizabeth was looking forward to the task. She hadn't been onstage since she was a child in London. She needed to prove to herself that she was capable. She trained for six weeks for the show World Enough and Time, which premiered on June 22, 1964. D. H. Lawrence, Shakespeare, and John Lennon's works were among those read. Despite the fact that she had a microphone, Burton wanted her to learn how to project her voice so that people at the back of the auditorium could hear her. When she messed up a line at the beginning of a serious poem, she said, "I'll begin again, I screwed up." Richard, who was also apprehensive, began reciting her lines, which caused them both to laugh so hard that they had to turn away from the audience. It could have gone very wrong from there, but Elizabeth proved herself to be a versatile actress capable of conquering both the stage and the cinema.

Richard began to spend more time with his daughter Kate as years passed and Sybil remarried (but he rarely saw Jessica, who spent her childhood in an institution). Kate Burton, who went on to star in Scandal and Grey's Anatomy, recalled a night when Elizabeth attempted to cook dinner for her, Michael, Christopher, Liza, and

83

.

Maria. Elizabeth decided to cook on the grill, and she got the steaks, which were of course the best money could buy, and she had her hair wrapped up in some kind of scarf, and she was sweating and huffing and puffing, and my father was getting very angry. The steaks are now on fire, and the baked potatoes are also on fire." After finishing Hamlet, Elizabeth and Richard made a cross-country train excursion from New York to California, stopping in Chicago to lay a rose on Mike Todd's grave. She read the script for Who's Afraid of Virginia Woolf? on the train. She couldn't sleep since she was so preoccupied with it. Ernest Lehman, the film's producer and screenwriter, recognized it was an unconventional choice, but he wanted her to play the lead.

Elizabeth and Richard were granted the unprecedented right to choose their director, which is quite unusual for any actor, and they chose Mike Nichols, whom they both knew and admired. Richard described him as "enthrallingly brilliant," and Elizabeth knew immediately that he was the ideal director for them and that they should trust him. She had never followed the rules, and Nichols was an unusual option. He was a humorist and director of three critically acclaimed stage comedies: Barefoot in the Park, Luv, and The Odd Couple. But he'd never directed a film before, and like Elizabeth, he was regarded to be too young and lacking in gravitas to pull off one of the decade's most important play adaptations on the big screen. He was only Elizabeth's senior. But he had campaigned both of them for the part, and the studio wanted to please their two stars. He'd met Elizabeth in Rome while she was working on Cleopatra, and Richard, a friend, had requested him to keep her company while he went out of town to finish filming The Longest Day. Nichols was taken aback by her candor.

Nichols adored Elizabeth and advised everyone who doubted her ability to play Martha to just wait and see. She was going to knock them out. Like Lehman, Nichols recognized that part of the film's draw would be audiences paying to see if Elizabeth could pull it off. Edward Albee, the writer, was among many who thought she was too young for the role, but he had no creative influence. Elizabeth portrayed a Big Sur artist who is a single mother. Morgan Mason, who played Elizabeth's young son, recalled speaking with the paparazzi stationed at the set's fence to protect the Burtons. One of them informed Mason, who was eight at the time, that he could bring his camera on set and play with it. Elizabeth, thirty-three, had already had a difficult year. Earlier that year, while Richard was filming The Spy Who Came in from the Cold in Dublin, she came to the aid of her lifelong friend and chauffeur Gaston Sanz. His adolescent kid appeared to have committed suicide in their village in the south of France.

When she arrived back in Dublin, she discovered that criminals had come into their hotel suite and taken property, including the wedding band she had given Mike. She wore it all the time since it was the only way she could recognize him after the plane accident. It was the most valuable piece of jewelry she owned. Then there was the issue of Elizabeth's citizenship. Elizabeth was born in London and has always held British citizenship. Her parents were both American citizens, hence she was born with dual citizenship. She wanted to renounce her American citizenship after marrying Richard. The move would save her hundreds of thousands of dollars in back taxes, and she had always felt a strong connection to the country where she was born. Things improved dramatically after she began working on Who's Afraid of Virginia Woolf? She was terrified of the challenge, but she knew she was prepared for it. Nichols was adamant on shooting the film in black and white.

The entire plot revolved around Elizabeth and Richard. Before filming began, everyone tried to court them, according to Ernest Lehman. "I hear that their agent, Hugh French, sent a quart—I repeat—a quart—to their dressing room on Tuesday." Night scenes were shot on the picturesque New England campus of Smith College in Northampton, Massachusetts. Because the film takes place late at night and Nichols wanted to capture the moonlight properly, they sometimes didn't start shooting until three or four a.m. Elizabeth walks in, turns on the light, throws her coat on a chair, misses it, and slurs, "What a dump." Seventy security personnel stood guard as the night scenes were shot. They were in Massachusetts for a month, and when Elizabeth became bored, she went to see What's New Pussycat?, which required ten police officers to accompany her.

Richard was nominated for Best Actor and Elizabeth was nominated for Best Actress at the 1967 Academy Awards for their roles in Who's Afraid of Virginia Woolf? They were filming The Comedians in France at the time, based on Graham Greene's novel about Haiti's tyrannical leader, Papa Doc Duvalier. Elizabeth had finished filming her scene, but Richard had to stay and do his. She had intended to attend the ceremony, but Richard informed her that he had a nightmare in which her jet crashed, and he made her feel bad for going in the first place, so she stayed by his side. He must have understood that she would win and he would not—she had already won the National Board of Review and the New York Film Critics Circle prizes. He was correct; she triumphed and he was defeated. Elizabeth was almost as terrified by their second picture. She was to portray Kate in Shakespeare's most renowned play, The Taming of the Shrew. It was Franco Zeffirelli's debut picture, and he had planned to cast Sophia Loren and Marcello Mastroianni, but when he saw Richard perform Hamlet, he knew he had to cast them together. Zeffirelli couldn't afford to pay Elizabeth a million dollars, but she and Richard decided it was worth it to co-produce the picture and defer their salary. It was their first time back in Rome since Cleopatra.

Monty died when she was filming The Taming of the Shrew in Italy. He was only 45 years old and it was July 1966. Elizabeth was informed that Monty had died of a heart attack at his New York mansion. He had spent much of his life as an addict and had suffered from a variety of ailments, including severe colitis and dysentery. Elizabeth chose not to attend Monty's burial in order to keep her mourning secret. She didn't seem surprised by the news. He was on too many pain relievers, she claimed (as was she). Truman Capote told her about Christmas shopping with Monty and how, after a couple of martinis at lunch, Monty excused himself to use the lavatory and returned as someone else. She'd never given up fighting for Monty. When she consented to appear in 1967's Reflections in a Golden Eye, she had one significant condition: Monty play her husband. He hadn't worked for four years since he was uninsurable. She knew how it felt because many studios felt the same way about her.

Monty was replaced by Marlon Brando after his death. "To me, they tap into and come from the same source of energy," Elizabeth explained. "They both have this acute animal sensitivity." Elizabeth had known Brando for a long time. He had personally handed the New York Film Critics Circle Award to her on the set of The Comedians in Cotonou, Benin, West Africa, where she was working. While Elizabeth was getting her makeup done, Brando came on set and cupped her bottom with both of his hands. "Marlon!" she exclaimed. Richard was doubtful of Brando and his motives, so he approached him and they got into an altercation that degenerated into each of them throwing blows at the other.

The third partner in their marriage was clearly alcoholism. Richard went through four stages when he was drinking: tipsy, when he was the kind and sober intellectual; buzzed, when he was amusing; drunk, when he was cruel; and truly drunk, when he passed out. His hands would shake so violently at times that he devised a makeshift pulley out of his belt. He'd take it off his waist and tie it over his wrist before passing it around the back of his neck, holding the glass with the hand connected to the belt and pulling the other end of the belt with his free hand to raise the glass to his lips. "For the last month now, with very few exceptions, she has gone to bed not merely sozzled or tipsy, but stoned," Richard wrote in his diary on January 13, 1969. "And I mean stoned, unfocused, unable to walk straight, talking like a demented child in a slow, meaningless baby voice..." The worst part is that it has turned me off to alcohol! ... The monotony of being in the presence of someone who requires you to repeat everything twice is like a physical pain in the stomach, unless I'm also intoxicated. If it were anyone else, I'd pack my belongings, flee to the hills, and live in a Trappist monastery, but this woman is my life." When Elizabeth was drunk, she became loud rather than rude, and when she was high on whatever pain medicine she was taking at the time, it was not as obvious as Richard's alcoholism.

Elizabeth debuted on the Motion Picture Herald's Top Ten Box Office Stars list in 1961, but she never appeared on it again until 1968. Boom! is a cult classic, although it was a commercial and critical flop when it was released in 1968. It was based on Tennessee Williams's The Milk Train Doesn't Stop Here Anymore, which was a flop on Broadway and considerably worse in the movies. Flora Goforth, the world's wealthiest woman, is dying slowly on her beautiful Mediterranean island, played by Elizabeth. Richard plays a wanderer who befriends wealthy women just before they die. The stunning scenery demonstrates that filmmaker Joseph Losey spared no money. The film was shot in an immense white home on a cliff two hundred feet above the Mediterranean in Sardinia. The house was ravaged by the elements, and during one especially powerful storm, Elizabeth's dressing room trailer rolled into the water. Fortunately, no one was inside.Boom! was also Elizabeth's brother Howard's first acting role. It was a fortunate coincidence. Howard and his wife, Mara, and their five children happened to be in town at the time, so when an actor failed to appear, Howard stepped in. He portrays the bearded boat captain who takes Richard to Goforth's island and then pushes him off the boat, forcing him to swim to shore.

One source of their dissatisfaction was their inability to live a normal life. When Elizabeth's small dogs got tar in their paws, she was distraught and screaming, so someone called a veterinarian. He just stood there transfixed when he came into the house and saw Elizabeth Taylor and Richard Burton sitting on the floor, with Elizabeth hunched over her dogs in tears. Elizabeth asked Bozzacchi to drive her to a town in Sardinia while they were filming Boom! so she could visit a diamond shop. He inquired if they should bring protection, to which she replied, "No, let's go on our own." They drove in his white Fiat instead of her flashy Rolls-Royce, but after a tight turn, both lanes of traffic were blocked by a car in the center of the road, and Bozzacchi yanked hard on the handbrake. Two men with hunting guns stood in front of them. When more men with firearms appeared, Bozzacchi quickly backed up the car and rushed away, returning to the hotel. They never found out if it was part of an abduction conspiracy, however Bozzacchi assumed someone at the hotel had informed them.

Elizabeth collaborated with Joseph Losey once more when he directed her in Secret Ceremony, a strange picture that costarred a young Mia Farrow and dealt with themes of rape, mental illness, and incest. Elizabeth admired Losey's unusual artistic perspective and recognized the fact that he had been blacklisted due to his Communist Party links. Because of Senator Joseph R. McCarthy's witch hunt, he had abandoned Hollywood for Europe. Throughout her life, Elizabeth was drawn to artists that questioned authority, such as Losey. Elizabeth and Richard remained aboard their yacht in the Thames while filming Secret Ceremony in London. She had always longed to be with her pets, but she was unable to do so due to quarantine protocols. Instead of having her dogs quarantined, she devised the extravagant plan of living with them on board their beautiful yacht.

Elizabeth went to the hospital in the summer of 1968 to have her uterus removed in an attempt to relieve her severe back pain. Her desire to have a biological child with Richard was dashed by the procedure. Richard believed Elizabeth placed too much reliance on her doctors and desired "shots, shots, shots, and pain relievers" rather than attempting to exercise and become healthier. He used to accuse Elizabeth of being a hypochondriac when he was in a bad mood. He once said to her that she was only sick when she wanted to be. Richard and Welch, according to Bozzacchi, were getting close. "I received a call from Richard at 3 a.m. He was crying, as if he was sad. Elizabeth and Claudye [Bozzacchi's wife] had gone on a holiday, and I was afraid Richard was crying because their plane had crashed! I hurried upstairs to Richard's apartment. He was inebriated and sobbing uncontrollably. When I unlocked the door to his bedroom, I found Raquel Welch naked on his bed. 'Gianni!' Richard burst into tears. 'I should never have hurt Elizabeth!' I have no idea what happened; I'd never seen somebody so inebriated. He was unable to stand. I jolted Raquel awake, assisted her in dressing, and led her to her room. Richard never informed me what happened or didn't happen that night, probably because neither he nor Raquel remembered anything."

On September 13, 1971, Richard wrote in his diary, "for breaking my contract to look after her forever, for letting her down with a bang (hysterical pun intended)... and for not realizing and demonstrating my full potential as husband, provider, lover, and all." We were "mutually self-destructive," according to Elizabeth. "Perhaps we loved each other too much." They knew, however, that their volatile relationship was a valuable commodity in and of itself, and they continued to benefit from it. They agreed to do Divorce His, Divorce Hers, a television movie about a marriage breakup, in 1972. It was shot in Rome and Munich and alternated between the husband's and wife's perspectives. This was due to the fact that neither Richard nor Elizabeth lived in Los Angeles or London for more than ninety days in a row because they did not want to pay taxes on their film income. Waris Hussein, the 34-year-old director of Divorce His, Divorce Hers, found himself in the midst of the most turbulent moment in the relationship of the world's most renowned marriage. Elizabeth hadn't even read the script; she'd agreed to do it only because Richard was on the board of Harlech TV, a Welsh television station that was funding the film. She was doing it for him as a favor, and he was doing it for Harlech. They shot at night on Via Condotti, where Richard had purchased Elizabeth's jewelry from Bulgari a decade before. "Suddenly," Hussein said, "the whole scene explodes into flash photography, lots of paparazzi, as Elizabeth gets out of the car, and it's like the Red Sea parting." She arrived two days early. On set, she sat enveloped in her fur coat, wondering where Richard was.

But they continued to put on the act of being a fashionable couple. Richard and Elizabeth had four-course lunches for friends from noon to three, which meant that little work was done after lunch. Hussein was filming a brunch scene once, and Elizabeth was pouring coffee into cups with no steam coming out. He requested a meeting with the person in charge of props. He once drunkenly told Gianni Bozzacchi that he was a millionaire not because of Elizabeth, but because of his own efforts. The next day, he had no recollection of it. Divorce His, Divorce Hers aired on February 6 and 7, 1973, to the worst possible reviews. According to Variety, watching it "holds all the joy of standing by at an autopsy." The Hollywood Reporter described it as "a boring, tedious study of a crumbling marriage between two shallow people." Except in your situation, I have generally mistreated women and exploited them to exercise my contempt. I battled like a fool to treat you the same way, but I failed... We're such damned idiots. Unfortunately, we are aware of it." Signed: "Ravaged love and loving Rich."

CHAPTER 12
The Loot: Elizabeth's Extraordinary Jewels

Elizabeth's jewelry is a scrapbook that captures the tale of her life and the intense, unmistakable love she shared with Richard. Even when their relationship was at its worst, she had incredible pieces of him to cling on to; perhaps she realized they wouldn't be together forever and needed something she could touch and feel to remind her of him. Her interest in jewels began when she was a child. She saw an exquisite colored-stone brooch in the window of a boutique in the Beverly Hills Hotel, near her father's art gallery, when she was twelve years old. She intended to purchase it for Sara for Mother's Day. She asked the store employee to hold the pin for her until she had enough money to purchase it. Even as a brilliant negotiator, she demanded a fair price. Elizabeth liked to be close to her jewelry at all times, so she kept it in a jewelry closet off her Bel Air home's dressing room. There were drawer banks with stacks of jewelry trays and drawers for earrings and bracelets. On the second floor, there was a small safe where all of the important jewels were kept for quick access. Other pieces were housed in a seven-foot safe at the ground-floor office. The extremely expensive jewelry was one of the reasons she required 24-hour security. Richard, who grew up poor, enjoyed purchasing expensive gifts for her almost as much as she enjoyed getting them. No one was more ecstatic, more delighted, than Elizabeth when she received a piece of jewelry, large or tiny, though she preferred the larger stones. Richard did not normally offer large gifts for Christmas and birthdays; he preferred surprises. Demi Moore awarded Elizabeth with the Council of Fashion Designers of America's renowned Lifetime of Glamour Award in 1998. Elizabeth believed it was strange that she was being handed such a significant honor after decades of being chastised by the closed-off fashion world.

Elizabeth had a varied and eccentric sense of style, and she loved clothes, though not nearly as much as she enjoyed jewelry. She donned Christian Dior, Chanel, and Balenciaga, and she popularized Halston caftans. She lacked a stylist, and her fashion sense was wild and extremely personal. She played with colors and patterns and was never entirely devoted to one designer, as Audrey Hepburn was to French designer Hubert de Givenchy, who produced her most iconic designs. Elizabeth recognized tremendous potential, and just as she helped enhance Bulgari's profile by adding part of her astronomical star power to the Italian jeweler, she helped make Valentino Garavani, also known as Valentino, a household brand. When she was in Rome filming Cleopatra in 1961, she asked the then-unknown Italian designer if he could make her an evening gown. She donned the magnificent white floor-length gown he had fashioned for the Spartacus premiere in Rome. Photos of her dancing with the film's star, Kirk Douglas, were widely circulated, and soon celebrities and socialites were demanding to wear Valentino. She and Valentino, who is now one of the world's most well-known and renowned couturiers, formed a lifetime connection. She began referring to him as "Rudy," after the gorgeous Italian actor Rudolph Valentino. Ward Landrigan, Sotheby's jewelry department chief, was in his twenties when he met Elizabeth and Richard and presented them with the most exquisite diamond he had ever seen. Richard spent $305,000 (about $2.5 million in today's currencies) for the Krupp, a 33.19-carat Asscher-cut stone owned by Vera Krupp, the ex-wife of Alfred Krupp, a Nazi war criminal whose family was the premier weapons producer during both world wars.

Elizabeth was on her hands and knees scouring the carpet for a misplaced present from Richard a few months later, in 1969, in the top-floor apartment of Caesars Palace in Las Vegas. La Peregrina, one of her most prized works, had gone after Richard had recently spent a fortune on it. In the late 1500s, La Peregrina, or "The Wanderer," was discovered in the Gulf of Panama and sent to King

Philip II. It was a Spanish Crown Jewel, and it can be seen in numerous photographs of the Spanish royal family. The pearl eventually made its way to France, where it was inherited by Charles Louis Napoleon Bonaparte, the future Napoleon III, president and emperor of France during the mid-1800s. The pearl was sold to the Englishman James Hamilton, Duke of Abercorn, and remained in their family until Richard purchased it at a Sotheby's auction for $37,000 (the equivalent of $290,000 today) as a Valentine's Day gift for Elizabeth.

During one of their frequent squabbles, Richard described Elizabeth's hands as "large, ugly, red, and masculine" that same year. "You really need to get me that 69-carat ring to make my ugly big hands look smaller and less ugly!" Elizabeth exclaimed the next morning. "That insult last night is going to cost me," he predicted. The diamond Elizabeth was referring to was a perfect 69.42-carat pear-shaped diamond that formerly belonged to the sister of Walter Annenberg, the billionaire publisher who served as the United States' ambassador to the United Kingdom during Richard Nixon's presidency. She believed the ring was so daring that she kept it in a bank vault rather than wearing it. When Elizabeth and Richard found out it was available, they requested Landrigan to come to Gstaad and show them around. Elizabeth loved anything she liked, and this diamond was no exception.

Elizabeth was particularly fond of Van Gogh, and she could stare at it for hours. He was the only artist she stated could make her cry just by gazing at his works. "There's something desperate, sad, and lonely," she explained. When the sea became rough, the workers rushed to remove the museum-quality paintings from the walls so they would not be harmed. Elizabeth's favorite bedroom on the yacht was furnished in white and yellow. She referred to the yacht as the "best toy." Richard joked that he could now bring his enormous book collection with him when they went. Elizabeth intended to attend

Princess Grace's Scorpio Ball wearing her new diamond. Cartier delivered three diamonds so that would-be thieves couldn't tell which were genuine. According to Bozzacchi, there were three identical boxes carried by three individuals who even looked alike.

Elizabeth wore a 69.42-carat pear diamond hung on a Cartier necklace at the Oscars in 1970, when she presented the Best Picture award. Richard enjoyed investigating the history of the things he purchased for his wife, and the tale behind the Taj Mahal drew him in. The inscribed heart-shaped table-cut diamond hangs from a gold neck chain set with cabochon rubies and old-mine cut diamonds and is set within a redstone and jade setting. According to legend, it was created during the Mughal period for Nur Jahan, the wife of Emperor Jahangir. Jahangir, Shah Jahan's father, is claimed to have inherited the stone and given it to his favorite bride, Queen Mumtaz Mahal. In her honor, Shah Jahan erected the Taj Mahal. The inscription "Eternal love 'til Death' " is carved into the stone. It is very probably the most romantic and one-of-a-kind piece in Elizabeth's magnificent collection. Surprisingly, Elizabeth persisted on loving her smallest piece of jewelry just as much as her largest. Richard paid $38 for a .042-carat diamond ring, which they dubbed the Ping Pong diamond. And she received the ring as her prize.

She had a sentimental attachment to a piece she had purchased for herself. When she was eighteen years old and married to Nicky Hilton, she met the Duke and Duchess of Windsor. Richard was making a film in Paris years later, when Le Scandale broke, and she got to know them. When King Edward VIII abdicated the British monarchy in 1936 to marry the twice-divorced American Wallis Simpson, the couple had become as well-known and contentious as the Burtons. They invited Elizabeth and Richard to their country property because they could relate to them and the uproar that their relationship had produced. Elizabeth observed Simpson was wearing a wonderful pin with three feathers and a gold crown composed of diamonds set in platinum, which was the Prince of Wales' insignia. When Elizabeth inquired about the royal insignia, Simpson replied, "Yes, and when Monty [Lord Mountbatten, a member of the royal family] came over, he took all the royal pieces back, but he missed this one." "I really gotta love them," Elizabeth remarked of the troubled marriage. After Simpson died in 1986, Elizabeth spotted the pin in a charity auction and thought to herself, "The Duchess wants me to have that." She was bidding on the phone while sitting by her pool with her family. She adored the piece and its history, but she was even more pleased that the proceeds will benefit the Pasteur Institute in Paris, a medical research center focused on AIDS and cancer research. She was bidding against someone who wanted it as much as she did, but not for the same reason. "I wanted it because I knew she wanted me to have it, it was like a spooky eerie thing. . . . So I kept on saying, 'More, more, yes, more, more. Yes, yes . . .'" She ended up paying $565,000. "The kids and everybody's looking at me, just staring at me like I'd flipped my wig." When she told her family the astronomical price, some of them threw themselves into the swimming pool.

CHAPTER 13
1973-1976: The End and the Beginning

Elizabeth began filming Ash Wednesday at the northern Italian ski resort of Cortina d'Ampezzo in May 1973. The plot revolves around a middle-aged woman who decides to undergo major plastic surgery in order to win back her straying spouse. It was another case of life mimicking art; Elizabeth was 41 years old and trying to cling to Richard, who followed her but was unhappy. Dominick Dunne, a producer on the film, recalled recommending that they have dinner with Andy Warhol one night. Elizabeth laughed at the concept at first. "That man made millions off of me!" she exclaimed, referring to Warhol's famous silkscreens that used her likeness without her permission. She was angry that they had helped him become a superstar. (He finally gave her a little lithograph that was not one of the originals, which she put in her Bel Air home's living room.) She finally consented to see him. Their booze-soaked evening went swimmingly until Elizabeth rose to use the ladies' room after dessert. She felt something hard under her sable coat as she rose from the red velvet bench. Warhol had hidden a tape recorder there.

Their relationship was a roller coaster, with them on and off for months. They recognized that chaos is always entertaining. She could never trust Richard, and for good reason: his adultery tore them apart before their divorce. Elizabeth's greatest concern was that Richard and Sophia Loren would work on a film together. Elizabeth left to begin filming The Driver's Seat in Rome, but she missed Richard. Gianni Bozzacchi recalled assisting Elizabeth in preparing for lunch at Loren and Ponti's villa. "They were trying to find a way back together," he recounted. While Elizabeth was getting dressed in the bathroom, Bozzacchi waited in Elizabeth's seven-room suite at the Grand Hotel. Finally, when she appeared, he couldn't disguise the expression on his face. Bozzacchi tried to console her, telling her how lovely she was even though she was wearing no makeup and was dressed in shorts and a T-shirt.

She was suffering from awful stomach aches in the late fall of 1973, and she was convinced she had cancer. She was taken to UCLA and underwent surgery to remove a benign ovarian cyst. Richard was still filming The Voyage when she urged him to "come back home." He left Italy with no luggage and raced to her bedside when she requested him to "come back home." Wynberg was fired on the spot. Richard informed her that he had quit drinking and that he had forgiven her for her relationship with Wynberg. Of course, he had his fair share of "cathartic infidelities." She accompanied Richard to a little village north of Sacramento to film The Klansman, and it was there that things began to fall apart once more. It was humiliating for Richard to ogle other women and flirt shamelessly in front of Elizabeth. He was fed up with her numerous illnesses, her entourage, and the business of being Elizabeth Taylor. They chose to spend more time apart from each other.

However, a month later, on April 26, 1974, they announced their separation. Elizabeth went to a courthouse near Gstaad two months later to complete it. Rowe-Beddoe's Elizabeth and Richard come to life in a story from the late 1960s, when they came to stay at his cottage in the English countryside. Elizabeth desired her favorite drink, Dom Pérignon. She headed over to the pub in the early afternoon and asked the bartender, who nearly fainted at the sight of her, whether they had any. When he told her they didn't, she dispatched her driver to London, an hour and a half away, to buy some. In February 1975, Wynberg, who was back in the picture, traveled to Russia with Elizabeth to film The Blue Bird. George Cukor directed the film, which was the first Soviet-American co-production during the Cold War. The actors, including Elizabeth, spent much of the shoot in bed, battling ailments ranging from the flu to amoebic dysentery. On August 14, 1975, Mary boarded an aircraft to Switzerland after receiving a telegram from Richard saying he wanted to visit her. Wynberg was fired yet again. She ran into Richard's arms, crying, and they both expressed how much they missed each other. They were officially reunited.

Elizabeth and Richard were still drinking excessively during their reconciliation, but something happened in October 1975 that convinced Elizabeth that she and Richard needed to remarry. They had been traveling all over the world, including to Johannesburg, South Africa, to attend a celebrity tennis event for charity. Gavin de Becker, now a celebrity security specialist, began his career working for Elizabeth and Richard during this time period. But Richard wasn't drinking at the time, according to de Becker, because he was on Antabuse, a drug that makes you sick if you drink. Elizabeth told de Becker one day that Richard had been drinking and that she was concerned. De Becker entered their hotel room and noticed Richard was in bad shape. He must have overdosed on Antabuse. De Becker leased a jet and flew in a doctor, who slammed an IV bag against the wall and drugged Richard. The doctor informed de Becker that Richard would not awaken for the next twenty-four hours.

In Botswana, Elizabeth and Richard met Chenina Sam, an Italian-Egyptian pharmacologist known as "Chen." Elizabeth and Sam quickly became close friends. She traveled back to London with them, and Elizabeth hired Sam as her PR despite her lack of expertise. It made sense, de Becker reasoned, because Sam was a pharmacist who could always assist her in obtaining the drugs she felt she required. She knew Richard despised gin, so whenever she felt he needed anything, she recalled giving Richard a small glass of gin to drink. She hoped he wouldn't consume too much of it, but he did. She hoped that a little wine would calm his frayed nerves, and her compassion for this guy she adored made his anguish excruciating to behold.

Richard was not the man she had married eleven years earlier; his health was failing and he was attempting to remain sober. "When one person recovers, the other person suffers greatly." So, despite the fact that Elizabeth had never had a relationship with Richard, they reconnected because he wasn't drinking. "There wasn't enough drama for her," de Becker explained. A health crisis transformed their life, however momentarily, in Botswana. "I am writing this for [Richard and] myself—while I still remember it," Elizabeth wrote in a lengthy diary entry. She assumed she had a cracked or broken rib, and when she went to have it X-rayed, she was told that she had scar tissue on her lungs from one of her illnesses. However, they may be far worse. "My eyes had seen hundreds of X-rays from every possible angle— but I had never, ever seen those spots." I didn't want to explain anything or go into too much depth with the doctors. I really wanted to see Richard." Elizabeth hoped he might want to marry again. "I'll carry you off on a white charger, but I'd prefer it if it were the other way around," she wrote. "I'm a hopeless romantic who fantasizes about being romantically swept away." Meanwhile, we'll be lovely and sweet—but one day, you son of a bitch, something will make you realize that you can't live without me and that you must marry me or your life would be incomplete. Both of us must be enthusiastic. I agree, don't stay in limbo for too long for both of our sakes. I love you with my life, and I want to make the most of my time here."

Christmas in 1975 was particularly terrible. Elizabeth's children recall Richard's binge drinking at its worst. Richard despised Christmas' sentimentality and consumerism, and the occasion brought out the worst in him. That Christmas, Richard met Suzy Hunt, a tall blonde who was twenty-seven years old and had recently married Formula One race-car driver James Hunt. Richard left a heartbroken Elizabeth at the Gstaad chalet and accompanied Hunt to New York to prepare for his performance in the play Equus. He informed acquaintances that now that he was (temporarily) sober, he had no idea why he and Elizabeth had married again. Elizabeth was resolved not to dwell in her loneliness, so she began a love engagement with Peter Darmanin, a thirty-seven-year-old advertising executive. They met on the dance floor at the Cave, a nightclub in Switzerland. He spent seven weeks at her chalet. Elizabeth and Richard met the next day at the Lombardy Hotel on East 56th Street. This was why she had been invited to New York in the first place. She arrived to find Richard standing next to Suzy Hunt at the hotel bar. He didn't appear to be himself.

Elizabeth and Richard were awarded their second divorce on July 29, 1976, less than 10 months after they married for the second time. "I love Richard with every fiber of my soul," she said to herself, "but we can't be together." "The only way for my father to survive, or continue to live," Kate Burton recalled of their second divorce, "was for him to be by himself." He was never alone, though. Elizabeth attended a preview of Equus before finally releasing Richard. Suzy Hunt was now the gatekeeper at Richard's dressing-room door, but Elizabeth saw an opening. "You were fantastic, Love," she scribbled in lipstick on his mirror, exactly as she did in BUtterfield 8: "You were fantastic, Love." The message remained there for several days.

CHAPTER 14
Wife of a politician

Elizabeth knew she'd never love anyone the way she loved Richard, and despite her disappointment at finding herself alone at forty-four, she refused to blame herself. She took charge of everything in her life. She was an everlasting optimist who thought her next great love was just around the corner. And in the summer of 1976, she met two potential suitors. The two new males in Elizabeth's life were diametrically opposed. Dinner with the Queen determined their fate in the end. One of them was a southerner called John Warner, who served as Secretary of the Navy under Richard Nixon and had recently divorced Catherine Mellon, an heir to the Mellon fortune. The other was Ardeshir Zahedi, Iran's ambassador to the United States and a fixture on Washington's social scene. He, like Warner, had previously married into a distinguished family; his first wife was the eldest child of Iran's shah, Mohammad Reza Pahlavi. When Elizabeth met Zahedi, he was forty-eight years old and attractive and worldly. His embassy parties were famous, and he was known for bringing journalists and Washington influencers jars of caviar and magnums of champagne to curry favor. But he was not looking to settle down, and he had been living as a bachelor since his divorce from Pahlavi in 1964.

Elizabeth fell hard and fast in love with Zahedi. Despite the fact that they had only been dating for a few months, she was considering marriage. However, the shah, Zahedi's former father-in-law and boss, had prohibited him from marrying Elizabeth during his lifetime. Though the shah was a moderate, the prospect of Iran's ambassador to the United States becoming Elizabeth's seventh trip down the aisle was too much to bear. And she was Jewish on top of that. Elizabeth would have been the stepmother to the Shah's grandchild if they had married. But Zahedi claimed that the actual reason they didn't marry was because he didn't want to get married again. He had been in love with Elizabeth since he met her in the 1954 film The Last Time I met Paris. "I invited her to my parties, and she would occasionally stay at the embassy." We were quite close friends, and I began to notice her with my daughter more and more. I grew fond of this lady and how amazing, bright, and domineering Elizabeth was." One of the final and most anticipated events was a Bicentennial supper sponsored by Queen Elizabeth II at the British embassy. It was jam-packed with celebrities and politicians, including President Gerald Ford and Bob Hope. But the dinner's host, British ambassador Sir Peter Ramsbotham, required assistance: Elizabeth Taylor would be attending and would require an escort. So he dialed his friend's number.

Warner married the sixth of her seven husbands five months after dining with the Queen, and she became the first major actress to marry a U.S. senator and migrate to Washington. In December 1976, they married on a farm hilltop. She was dressed to the knees in a cashmere gown and a wool and silk knit coat with a gray fox collar and matching hat. She was running late as usual. Following their marriage, Elizabeth invited Warner to her chalet in Gstaad, Switzerland, to meet Richard. She wanted to introduce Richard to her husband, a gorgeous politician. When Warner answered the door, there stood outside Richard Burton in a large fur coat. "I see you've made yourself at home," Richard replied, his dramatic voice booming. "Do you realize you're wearing my sweater?" Elizabeth had instructed Warner to take everything he desired from Richard's old closet to keep warm. After a little pause, Richard, ever the theatrical, walked inside and exclaimed, "Hell, keep it all!" She knew Warner planned to run for Senate in 1978, and she believed she would be a tremendous help to him. There had never been a movie star as a Senate candidate's wife before, and voters were eager to see her. She grew to like campaigning, and people were taken by how personable and down-to-earth she could be. Looking back, Zahedi believes the reason they married so quickly was because "Warner wanted her to be helpful and this is why he rushed." Elizabeth never questioned his motivations. She was traditional; this is what you do for your husband. She campaigned for two months, making up to six stops every day throughout Virginia. She traveled wherever she was informed she could help, including rural places in the coal area of southwest Virginia. Her work ethic was evident from the age of nine when, after a fifteen-minute procession ended and the driver of the car she was in shut off the motor, she insisted on turning it back on so they could circle back and do it all over again. After all, the procession was just seven blocks long and she had acquired new clothing for it.

Most Senate contests last one to one and a half years. Despite her huge celebrity power, Warner lost the Republican primary to Richard Obenshain, who died tragically in a plane crash—an occurrence that upset Elizabeth since it reminded her of losing Mike Todd. Warner took over as the Republican nominee after Obenshain, and he had less than three months to win. Elizabeth went into overdrive, maintaining a grueling schedule with only Sundays off. She felt revitalized after the humiliation of yet another failed marriage to Richard. People had come to see her, but they stayed to listen to him. According to one campaign sticker, "See Elizabeth, vote for John." But Elizabeth was too strong a force to be a supporting character, and she wasn't the type to hold her tongue. Warner and his campaign staff urged her to change her identity. Her celebrity would lure people to campaign rallies, but her Hollywood lifestyle could harm him. This was in the immediate aftermath of Watergate, and Warner was concerned about maintaining appearances. Attempting to change who she was did not work. She was gaining weight quickly. There was so much travel, and fast food was the quickest option on the campaign trail. She famously choked on a piece of fried chicken at a campaign stop because it was her first chance to eat all day. Elizabeth sat next to her husband in a drab mustard yellow outfit with an olive green headband and unruly shoulder-length hair in a 1978 campaign interview. She appeared to be half asleep. She was bent over with her arms crossed on her lap, clearly struggling to get through the interview. The question hit Elizabeth like a slap in the face, and you can see her recoil.

Alan Simpson, a Republican senator who served with Warner and remembered how difficult Elizabeth's life was in Washington, remembered how difficult Elizabeth's life was in Washington. "We went to galas and fundraisers, me and my wife, and Senator Warner and his wife," Simpson explained. "She was completely out of her element. I believe she tried her best; it was just so unusual for her. My wife described life in the Senate, and she attempted to assist Elizabeth understand life in the fast lane in politics, where there is ego and self-aggrandizement and adornment, among other things. "I thought she handled her difficult situation admirably." But Elizabeth understood the world of power and politics because she had grown up in Hollywood, but Warner did not treat her as a true partner.

Elizabeth was named Woman of the Year in 1977 by the Harvard Hasty Pudding Theatricals, a student group. She was delighted to be recognized, and she planned to give an acting workshop while she was there. She had a meeting with thirty kids. "I love the parts that aren't me, where I can scream and tear up the scenery," she explained. She stood on a balcony with one of her stepchildren and Warner before receiving the trophy. After Warner was elected, she exacted sweet vengeance by wearing her purple Halston pantsuit proudly to a luncheon hosted by Republican ladies to thank her for her assistance. She had never been afraid to express herself. She made the courageous decision five months before their wedding to give herself as a hostage in exchange for the more than one hundred Air France passengers being detained by terrorists at Entebbe Airport in Uganda. The plane took off from Tel Aviv, was seized by Palestinian and German terrorists, and was forced to land in Uganda.

Though her offer to trade herself for the hostages was rejected, she did play a hostage in Victory at Entebbe, an ABC broadcast reenactment of the Israeli rescue raid. She was noticeably more forward-thinking than her husband. Warner opposed the Equal Rights Amendment, whereas Elizabeth did. He did say she helped broaden his perspective. "She's worked since she was 10 years old, and she's worked hard... And [their marriage] had been a humbling experience for me."

Elizabeth may not have called herself a feminist, but she was unquestionably one. Beyond the apparent equal rights message in National Velvet, her daring and gritty film choices demonstrate her interest in feminism and social justice: A Place in the Sun (1951), released twenty-two years before Roe v. Wade made access to a legal and safe abortion a constitutional right; in Giant (1956), Elizabeth plays Leslie Benedict, a woman who forces the white ranchers' doctor to intervene and save the life of a dying Mexican child and who raises her son to be a feminist; and in Suddenly, Last Summer (1959), Elizabeth plays Catherine Ho.

Elizabeth was adamant that women should be paid the same as men for the same work. She stated that she was "very proud of women who do professional work while also balancing family life." When Warner listened to her, she was able to effect genuine change. During the campaign, the governor of Virginia invited Warner and Elizabeth to lunch at the Governor's Mansion in Richmond, which they gladly accepted despite the fact that there was a foot of snow on the ground. The airport was closed when Warner and Elizabeth arrived. As a result, they rode the bus to Richmond. She vanished inside the airport and reappeared after only a minute. "Which of you guys has a dime?" Some women's restrooms required payment before they could be used. Nobody had any money. As they sped to the Governor's Mansion, Warner ordered the governor's driver to meet the bus and activate sirens. When they eventually arrived, Elizabeth jumped out of the car and nearly ran over the governor's wife on her way to the restroom.

Meanwhile, Elizabeth was trying to balance being one of the world's most famous people, a new marriage, and her four children: Michael, who was twenty-six; Chris, who was twenty-four; Liza, who was twenty-one; and seventeen-year-old Maria. She had to fire an old friend, John Springer, her longtime publicist. Chen Sam stayed, and lived with Elizabeth and Warner. "John [Warner] wanted very understated work," Sam said diplomatically. "No Hollywood types," which included Springer. After Warner won his Senate seat in 1978, he hosted a fundraiser breakfast at their Georgetown mansion and invited twenty-five senators and dozens of lobbyists, who paid two thousand dollars a seat. Their housekeeper came down just as the group was leaving and said that Elizabeth wanted to know if breakfast was still warm.

But Elizabeth was growing desperately unhappy in Washington. Warner was a workaholic who rarely missed a vote in the Senate. When the campaign was over, she felt completely abandoned by him. "I had no function anymore, not even as an ornament." Far from friends in Los Angeles, she ate and drank at home alone, ultimately gaining more than forty pounds. "Every time Liz Taylor goes into McDonald's, the numbers on the sign outside start changing," joked Joan Rivers, who relentlessly fat-shamed her. "When she looks up and sees five billion, she thinks it's her weight." She found herself in a sort of "domestic Siberia," she said. Before the campaign, she was asked by a journalist if she thought that their marriage could withstand it if he won. "I'll tag along," she said. But she soon learned that she could not go with her husband to Capitol Hill every day. And she also did not know that when a senator is not voting they are often on the road campaigning for colleagues who are up for reelection or going back to their states to hold events with voters to get reelected themselves. She made friends with Senator Howard

Baker and his wife, and even with Republican senator Barry Goldwater, whom she enjoyed teasing. But she was a passionate and creative person who had nowhere to put her energy, no way to be useful.

But watching Elizabeth's spiral into serious drunkenness and painkiller addiction was terrible for her family. According to Chris Wilding, his mother truly wanted to be a supporting wife, but what it entailed "came as a bit of a rude awakening." Richard had always been opposed to drug use. Because he had grown up with alcohol as the workingman's panacea, he saw it as aristocratic. Elizabeth felt liberated after their divorce to do drugs and take medications without disguising them. Elizabeth and Richard were still in one another's lives, even though she wasn't talking about him as often as she used to, just like any divorced couple trying to co parent their children. Liza always called Richard her "dad," and Mike Todd, whom she never met because he died when she was young, her "father." Despite the fact that they were not a couple, she relied on him to be a stabilizing presence in her life. "You don't look a day over 75, stay young at heart, and just because it's your birthday, there's no need to get pissed," she said in 1982. I adore you, your double ex-wife. Elizabeth." Elizabeth and Richard would be inseparable, not only because of their children, but also because of their undying love for one another. Tivey recalls meeting Richard for the first time before Liza married Hap Tivey. They were driving to Gstaad and stopped at Richard's house outside of Geneva.

And Elizabeth yearned for the freedom she experienced with Richard. Before John Springer was fired in August 1977, he counseled Elizabeth not to fund organizations advocating for gay rights. Several organizations had written to her, requesting her assistance in their efforts against Anita Bryant, a gospel singer who led a fight against a 1977 ordinance in Miami-Dade County that prohibited job and housing discrimination based on sexual orientation. Bryant became a well-known figure and part of a national backlash against gay rights when the law was overturned. A Field poll conducted in September 1978 revealed that 61 percent of California voters supported banning gay teachers, which was consistent with national attitudes at the time. Elizabeth would have preferred to speak out against Bryant, especially when hard-fought homosexual rights were under threat, but she felt she couldn't since she was the wife of a Republican senator. Every journey she took had to be approved by Warner and his team. In September 1979, she was invited to be the honorary guest at the Cairo Film Festival. On September 14, 1979, Aaron Frosch wrote her a concerned letter: "I am informed that you will shortly depart for Egypt for a visit to Egypt and Israel." Is John aware of your plans, and does he feel that a trip to both nations would be detrimental to his career?" She went regardless.

She resolved to reinvent herself at the age of 49. She visited the Palm-Aire Spa in Florida with her renowned hair stylist pal Maury Hopson. Their cabin was dubbed "BUtterfield Ate Too Much." "She asked me to be her friend and help her get through it... I don't think she realized what she was getting herself into... 'I'm drinking this stuff like it's vodka,' she exclaimed as she drank from a water bottle." They stayed for three weeks and she shed 22 pounds. "She suddenly became Elizabeth Taylor again," Hopson explained. Warner was initially uncomfortable with her gay acquaintances, of which she had many, but she, he claims, helped broaden his mind. "She persuaded me. We drove to Rock Hudson's place, and he introduced us to a gentleman who was definitely his boyfriend, which made me a little uncomfortable." Welles was the first to sign on, and Hier wanted to get Elizabeth but didn't know how. He recognized Warner because they had collaborated on a bill that ensured there was no statute of limitations on Nazi war crimes. He forwarded the script to Warner, who placed it on Elizabeth's nightstand. She snatched it up and sobbed all night. "I've got to do this," she declared. A few days later, she called Hier and introduced herself as Mrs. Warner to the person who answered the phone.

Genocide won an Oscar, and at a dinner in her honor in 1980, she delivered a foreshadowing speech about the risks of forgetting the Holocaust. "Today, a whole generation is growing up that does not know this, has no memory of these events, and has no terms of reference to know how close we all came to the final curtain," she explained. "Worse, new ominous voices can be heard around this new generation, seeking to pollute their minds, corrupt their values, and undermine their future." Anti-Semitism is on the rise in Europe and the United States. Haters are vying for office, pitting whites against blacks and Christians against Jews." The audience erupted in raucous applause. Elizabeth Taylor had returned, no longer disguised in drab garb and no longer playing a supporting part. Now that she had rediscovered herself, she resolved to do something she had never done before. "In our final months together, she came to me and said there's a play I'd like to do," Warner explained. The play was Lillian Hellman's The Little Foxes, and at the age of 49, and after appearing in over fifty films, she faced one of her greatest anxieties. She was well aware that she still had a lot to learn about performing on stage. A red light in the theater, for example, is your cue to make your entrance. However, at a movie studio, it means to stop what you're doing and remain motionless. "She would freeze," her co-star Dennis Christopher said, "and she needed people to tell her to go like a little girl." That's how deeply embedded it was in her."

Austin Pendleton, the director of The Little Foxes, first met Elizabeth for dinner while she was still married to Warner. Pendleton recalls how strongly Elizabeth was affected by the assassination attempt on Ronald Reagan in 1981. During rehearsals, she informed him she intended to run a full-page ad in the first part of the New York Times advocating for gun control legislation, which enraged Warner. "That was a sharp turn for the worse in their relationship," Pendleton explained. She saw no problem with what she was doing. Following the assassination of Robert F. Kennedy in 1968, she persuaded one hundred other celebrities to sign a full-page ad in the New York Times, which she paid for, advocating for stricter gun control laws. Warner had always known she did not share his conservative political views, she reasoned. She did it anyway because she'd had enough. "I willingly and happily adapt myself to my husband's lifestyle." I can be pushed and shoved, and it's okay because I'm tough as nails. "I admit that if I'm pushed too far, even by my husband, something snaps inside me and the relationship ends."

"He knows he wasn't the love of my life," she told the New York Times in 2002, after having had decades to dwell on her seventh marriage. And, while I wasn't the love of his life, we were in love." She and Warner stayed in each other's lives till she died. Her friendship with him aided her in achieving what would become her biggest and most lasting legacy. A few months after their divorce, Elizabeth's children called Warner and asked if he might go up to New York and surprise their mother for Christmas. So he spent the morning in Washington with his family before flying to New York for the evening. Her children had not informed Elizabeth of his impending visit. They placed him in the middle of her living room, wrapped in a red gift. When she came out of her bedroom at noon, she noticed this massive parcel and said, "What is this???" But the end of every marriage carries a certain melancholy, and Elizabeth was not capable of lying about it. When Warner remarried in 2003, he called Elizabeth from outside the church to let her know. "I'm happy he's remarried," she said. "I hope he's better to his new wife than he was to me."

CHAPTER 15
Creating an Empire

Elizabeth treated her hair stylists, particularly her dear friend José Eber, as if they were family. She'd been through near-death experiences and seven marriages, and she wasn't about to be rushed for anyone. She went out to supper with Hamilton, and even though Connery had left, the table was packed with other friends. A dinner attendee informed Elizabeth about 1:00 a.m. that photographers had captured images of her sunbathing in her underwear. The celebrations were deafeningly quiet. Elizabeth began questioning everyone at the hotel until she discovered the name of a photographer who had been seen close that day with a telephoto lens on his camera. She demanded that he be brought to her right away. Elizabeth was restoring her independence. She was still taking pain relievers and sleeping drugs, but she was drinking less, sometimes not at all, and she felt in perfect control of her life at times. She'd lost weight (though it was still a struggle), and she started wearing slim-fitting trousers with her jet-black hair pushed high and her makeup applied professionally. She did her own makeup and spent extra time on her eyes, combining several hues with artistic skill and consuming at least an hour. She always puts on cosmetics before taking a bath and getting ready. Her helper would breathe a sigh of relief when she was running late and in the bath since it meant she was almost ready.

In the late 1980s and early '90s she was enjoying her life. Besides Hamilton, she dated a wide range of men, including the Pulitzer Prize–winning journalist Carl Bernstein. She wanted to keep their relationship private, and some of her friends never even met Bernstein. He dated other celebrities, including Bianca Jagger, but what they had in the mid-1980s was more than a fling. He told Elizabeth that she had helped him discover who he was. According to Tim Mendelson, Elizabeth ended it when she found out that he had told people about their relationship, which was meant to be kept a secret. She never stopped looking for love. The director David Lynch described the first time he met Elizabeth, at the Academy Awards in 1987, where she was presenting the award for Best Director. He was nominated for Blue Velvet, but Oliver Stone took the award home for Platoon. At superagent Swifty Lazar's famous after-party at Spago, Lynch was summoned to John Huston's back-room table, where Huston was sitting with Elizabeth.

In the early 1980s, while Elizabeth was playing in The Little Foxes, Jeffrey Katzenberg was at Paramount Studios, and he wanted her to star in Terms of Endearment alongside Debra Winger. He called her agent to make the proposition, but Katzenberg declined because he wanted to see Elizabeth in person first. Elizabeth was well aware that she would not be able to reprise her part as Martha in Who's Afraid of Virginia Woolf? That was difficult due to Hollywood's deeply rooted ageism and sexism. "My career vanished," she confided in a friend. "They're not looking for the same things anymore." And she had no desire to be a character actress; she had no desire to age gracefully as an actress. She worked for enjoyment on occasion. In a 1992 episode of The Simpsons, she delivered Maggie's first words: "Daddy." Normally, the room was virtually empty before recording, but this time the entire cast and crew had gathered at the recording stage to witness her. She walked in wearing the Krupp and holding her beloved white Maltese, Sugar. "I think I did about thirty takes, even though we probably didn't need that many," Simpsons writer Al Jean stated. When Jean exclaimed, "That's enough," she said, jokingly, "Fuck you!" Everyone in the room burst out laughing.

She felt as if she didn't belong at times. And she had an uncanny capacity to identify others who felt like outsiders or were struggling. Lesley-Anne Down, her co-star in A Little Night Music, was one of those folks. Down was embroiled in a high-profile custody dispute with Exorcist filmmaker William Friedkin. Years later, Down needed to get away from the media glare that surrounded her divorce. Elizabeth did not hesitate when she told her what she was going through and how frightened she was about losing custody of her two-and-a-half-year-old kid. "You're coming to me," she announced. "You can stay for as long as you want." Down stayed for three weeks, bringing her son, boyfriend, and mother with her. Elizabeth enjoyed caring for others, but she yearned for the simple pleasures of life, such as her family and her pets, notably Sugar, whom she carried with her everywhere. She also adored Alvin the parrot, whom Chris Wilding referred to as his mother's "principal sidekick" for a while and who could frequently be spotted perched on her shoulder in the 1980s. Bradley Anderson, Elizabeth's friend, remembered Alvin's eloquence. "It could, for example, do a Richard Burton impression." You'd be sitting in Elizabeth's bedroom, talking to her, when you hear Richard's booming voice: 'Elizabeth.'"

When Elizabeth and Carol Burnett were filming a picture together, a studio official came to see the set. Elizabeth, Burnett, and the executive were seated in Elizabeth's hotel suite when Elizabeth let Alvin out of his cage, and he excitedly soared around the room. Eventually, Alvin landed on the executive's shoulder. Elizabeth's extravagant lifestyle was expensive, and Chen Sam saw that Elizabeth had a cash-flow problem. Despite having one of the world's most precious jewelry and art collections, she lived lavishly. Elizabeth realized her worth from a young age and recognized that she was a brand. But it was Sam who pushed her to consider making a scent and set up a meeting with beauty professionals to make that happen. But it was Elizabeth who founded her celebrity perfume business, and it was Elizabeth who realized she could monetize on her reputation in unprecedented ways. No movie star had done one effectively since Zsa Zsa Gabor's Zig Zag, but Sam understood that ladies all over the world aspired to look and smell like Elizabeth. When they met at a dinner party in Paris, Coco Chanel, famous for the classic scent Chanel No. 5, insisted on doing one. "Elizabeth, movies do not last forever," Chanel replied. Perfume is eternal. "Promise me you'll make a perfume."

Elizabeth introduced Passion in 1987, and it quickly became a tremendously famous fragrance. Elizabeth wanted to be a part of every element of its production, from the perfume itself, dubbed "the juice" in the business, through the packaging and marketing. She was the first major celebrity to properly harness the power of her own brand in this manner, and she was a perfectionist when it came to anything bearing her name. After the popularity of Passion, Elizabeth Arden officials spent more than a year attempting to convince Elizabeth to create a follow-up fragrance. However, she considered Passion to be her defining aroma and did not believe a second perfume was necessary. Carlos Benaim, a renowned fragrance who worked on Polo by Ralph Lauren, paid Elizabeth a visit in Bel Air to persuade her differently. He arranged ten numbered bottles on a table and asked her to choose her three favorite fragrances. She opted for strong perfumes such as tuberose and jasmine. She stated that she preferred the aroma of the narcissus flower, and he assured her that they could develop a perfume she would enjoy. White Diamonds was born, which would go on to become one of the most successful scents of all time, with over $1.5 billion in sales.

She needed to approve the marketing plans after she authorized the scent, and she had a strong say in them. White Diamonds' elegant and cinematic black-and-white commercial was shot in Acapulco, and it begins with a private plane arriving on a beach and hordes of photographers rushing to capture Elizabeth. The screen flashes with images of sculpted males playing a card game. Elizabeth walks over to them in an off-the-shoulder white gown and says, "Not so fast," as she removes one of her massive diamond drop earrings and throws it on a mound of money on the table. "These have always brought me good luck." Her perfume line was so successful that it earned her significantly more money than her films, and White Diamonds is still in the top 10 celebrity scents. Her achievement, however, did not come easily. There will always be issues when there is that much money at stake. Elizabeth was required to appear in court with her ex-boyfriend, Henry Wynberg. He alleged she violated a contract they signed in 1977, a decade before Passion, to split 30% of net income from cosmetics marketed under her name. They finally struck an out-of-court settlement after four years, and no money was involved, according to another of Elizabeth's lawyers, Neil Papiano. "It means I'm vindicated, and it proves the perfume, Passion, is something I worked for a year and a half for," Elizabeth remarked after the agreement was reached. It has absolutely nothing to do with Henry Wynberg."

The legal victory came shortly after she almost died in 1990, when she was fifty-eight. She was hospitalized with pneumonia at St. John's Hospital in Santa Monica. She was placed on a ventilator and put in the intensive care unit. Infectious disease specialist Dr. David Ho consulted on the case and said that it was diffuse pneumonia of both lungs. This time the tabloid had gone way too far with their front-page story: "LIZ DOCS FURIOUS. SHE'S BOOZING IT UP IN THE HOSPITAL." Her lawyers cited another story with the headline: "LIZ'S BEAUTIFUL FACE RAVAGED BY KILLER DISEASE. DOCTORS ORDER SUICIDE WATCH AFTER THEY FINALLY DIAGNOSE THE MYSTERY ILLNESS." She filed a $20 million libel suit in 1990, which was settled a year later. She won an apology and an undisclosed sum of money after her medical records were made available to the Enquirer, proving the story was false.

She experienced another setback after that victory, but she was prepared for it. She knew that not every fragrance would be like Passion and White Diamonds because she had gone through so much in her life. She released Black Pearls in 1996, and while it did not perform well, she was not about to give up. Elizabeth's final on-screen appearances were in 1996, when she appeared in four consecutive primetime CBS television shows to promote Black Pearls. The premise was that she was looking for her missing black pearl necklace in each episode. Then, in the early 2000s, Elizabeth decided to create a Gardenia scent. She informed Tamara Steele, an Elizabeth Arden executive she had worked closely with for years, that she adored the fragrance since she used to use it in Puerto Vallarta while she was married to Richard. But she turned down every fragrance scented with gardenias that Steele offered her. Finally, Elizabeth requested that someone go into her garden and select a gardenia. She pressed it to Steele's nose. Creating a fragrance requires both art and science. There is a distinction between the aroma of a fresh flower and that of a cut bloom. Steele determined that capturing the exact aroma of a gardenia from Elizabeth's garden would be the only way to make her happy. Gardenia did not sell nearly as well as White Diamonds or Passion, but it was a labor of love.

When they were formulating the fragrance Forever Elizabeth, which was introduced in 2002, she requested that the packaging match the hue of the Van Cleef & Arpels oval-cut 8.9-carat ruby ring that Richard had packed in her stocking one Christmas. Violet Eyes was released two decades after White Diamonds.When Elizabeth went on scent tours, she had a staff go ahead of time to the place she was visiting to scout the greatest suites in the top hotcls. It was almost as if we were getting ready for a presidential visit. When they rented her a suite, they called her "Mrs. Norman Maine," like Judy Garland's role in A Star Is Born. But Elizabeth was keeping a life-changing secret from everyone. Elizabeth went somewhere alone during every single perfume tour, no matter how she felt, and this time no members of the press were invited. Thesc trips, when no one was looking, changed her life.

CHAPTER 16
Searching for Neverland

Elizabeth's seventh and last walk down the aisle took place on October 6, 1991. Larry Fortensky, a construction worker twenty years her junior, was the most peculiar of her husbands. She knew Michael Jackson, who graciously agreed to hold the wedding at his Neverland Ranch, 120 miles north of Los Angeles. The wedding was a mix of business and pleasure for Elizabeth. She established The Elizabeth Taylor AIDS Foundation (ETAF) with the proceeds from the $1 million sale of wedding images to People magazine. The guests were greeted with a large sign that said, "NO CAMERAS." In 1988, Elizabeth met Fortensky during her second visit to Betty Ford. He'd been jailed for DWI multiple times and had used his Teamsters Union insurance to go to Betty Ford. "We were at our most vulnerable," Elizabeth recalled of their first encounter. "In therapy, they knock you down, kick the s*** out of you, and then give you the tools to build yourself back up." Larry was quite protective of me. He later informed me that there were occasions when he wanted to kill the counselor." Fortensky, aged 39, grew up in Stanton, California, as the eldest of seven children in a working-class household. He dropped out of high school and was divorced twice. He had never flown before meeting Elizabeth. His job as a construction worker only added to his allure. He even continued to work after they were married.

The pair exchanged vows beneath a white gazebo on Jackson's 2,700-acre Santa Ynez Valley home. One photographer leaped out of a helicopter, pulled his parachute, and appeared to be gliding toward the altar, while the 160 high-profile guests, including Nancy Reagan and Brooke Shields, gazed in awe. He was cruising at a low altitude with a camera connected to his helmet, hoping to catch a glimpse of Michael Jackson. He appeared to be aiming for Mrs. Reagan at one point. Security personnel emerged from the woods, their rifles drawn. As the parachutist fell to the ground, one of them grabbed his legs. They ripped off his helmet and started searching him for bombs and weapons. It all happened in less than thirty seconds, and then he was gone. Reagan was immobile. Eight years as first lady had evidently prepared her for this.

Elizabeth, aged 49, arrived an hour late and dressed in a pale yellow $25,000 Valentino gown; her mother, Sara, sat in the front row in a wheelchair. Jackson accompanied her down the aisle on one side, and Michael Wilding Jr. on the other. José Eber, her hairstylist, was the best man. Elizabeth recognized the ridiculousness of the situation. She later apologized to star journalist Baz Bamigboye, who was one of the reporters leaning out of a helicopter on a harness to obtain a peek of the wedding. She was surrounded by aides who, according to Williamson, were overprotective of her—despite the fact that Elizabeth obviously wanted her employees to function as buffers and protectors between her and everyone else—and who didn't take Fortensky seriously. They would endure this marriage as they did her prior partnerships. Jackson danced with Elizabeth at the reception, while Shields had to dance with Fortensky. "As soon as we started dancing, I went over to Michael and Elizabeth and asked, 'Can I cut in?'" So I simply danced with Michael and handed her over to her husband." Shields spent the night feeling sorry for Elizabeth. She remembered how much Elizabeth loved the Heath Bar Crunch ice cream cake and how fast to laugh, but their wedding was the furthest thing from personal and private.

Elizabeth was Michael's closest celebrity relationship. He invited her to one of his shows, and they met. She had brought numerous friends, but they couldn't see the theater clearly and had to leave early. Michael advised that he pay her a visit one day. That sounded excellent to Elizabeth. Jackson had been abused by his father, and Elizabeth felt pity for him. She knew what it was like to be used for money and fame by your family. Elizabeth was described by Jackson as "a warm cuddly blanket that I love to snuggle up to and cover myself with." Fortensky was very protective and caring of Elizabeth early in their marriage, but by the end of it, five years later, they no longer shared the same bedroom. Most of her acquaintances believed he was boring and unsuitable for someone as colorful as his wife.

She took Fortensky to places he would never have seen otherwise. Her close friend, media billionaire Malcom Forbes, agreed to allow her and Fortensky to stay in his Moroccan home for their honeymoon. In 1992, Disneyland closed for the night to commemorate her 60th birthday, and a thousand of her friends were invited. Columns of violet and yellow balloons and a violet carpet at the castle entryway adorned the famed amusement park. Among the guests were Cindy Crawford, Richard Gere, David Bowie, Iman, and Carrie Fisher, as well as Disney CEO Michael Eisner, who led Elizabeth and Larry throughout the night. The tremendous media coverage gave the impression that it was a royal wedding. Guests were transported from the parking lot to the gates by horse-drawn carriages, and fireworks exploded high over Sleeping Beauty's castle.

Elizabeth and Fortensky appeared to be happy that night at Disneyland, but fractures in their marriage were already showing. She had given him a makeover and highlighted his hair, taught him proper manners, and even arranged for him to take speech classes. In public, Elizabeth was normally stoic, but she could be vulnerable when she remembered certain people. Jorjett Strumme was aware of how emotional she could become. Elizabeth, Fortensky, and Strumme traveled to London to see Richard Burton's relatives, who had come to have lunch with her. "We're in a large private dining room when Richard's Welsh family begins singing, and it's absolutely beautiful." She was at the head of the table, and I was in the center, and I was choking back tears as I stared up at her. We met eyes and both burst out crying." Sara died in 1994, at the age of 89.

But Elizabeth did not cry for a year after her mother died. A photograph from her mother's home appeared in her office in 1995. It was a photo of her with her mother from the 1960s that had her sobbing for an hour. After that day, when she sobbed after viewing a snapshot of her younger self with her mother, she and Fortensky were on the verge of divorce. Fortensky kept contacting Elizabeth after they split up, saying, "Elizabeth, I want to come home." Even after their marriage ended in 1996, Elizabeth continued to look after him. She gave him money in her will, and they chatted about once a month following their divorce. "Dear Larry," she wrote in an undated letter. I've been thinking about you a lot recently, and I'm worried about you. I'm not sure why—it's just one of my feelings.

The circumstances surrounding Elizabeth's connection with Michael Jackson were complicated. Jackson was the target of many sexual abuse allegations and police investigations beginning in 1993, with an indictment on ten felony offenses ranging from child molestation to kidnapping. His case went to trial in 2005, and it became a media circus, partly because he was one of the most famous individuals in the world at the time, but also because of his strange behavior, which included showing up to court late in his pajamas. He was cleared of all charges, but suspicion lingered. Elizabeth never believed it and stayed steadfast in her devotion to him. Charlie Nicholson, who worked for Elizabeth, said he saw her with Jackson in the late 1980s. She was hand-feeding him salad as they sat at the dining room table. She was willing to go to any length for him, and she did. Elizabeth organized a one-woman intervention for Michael in 1993. She traveled to Mexico City, where he was performing, and accompanied him to his private dressing area, where she persuaded him to seek therapy. She had already called Elizabeth Arden CEO Joe Spellman and informed him that she required a two-bedroom jet to transport a guest.

Jackson was in the midst of a professional and personal crisis at the time. Because of the child sex abuse allegations against him, he abruptly canceled the "Dangerous" tour, and PepsiCo terminated his endorsement arrangement. Bertram Fields, his attorney at the time, stated that his painkiller addiction had become all-consuming: "He was barely able to function adequately on an intellectual level." I'm not going to go into detail about his specific symptoms, but they were noticeable." Members of Jackson's family, according to Alon, were enraged with Elizabeth because they did not want him to acknowledge his addiction. Jackson's life was so tightly controlled that he had to get his own passport from his head of security. Michael's experience in treatment, like Elizabeth's at Betty Ford, was humbling, as he learned how to handle a vacuum cleaner and other menial activities. Despite all of Jackson's planning and deception, his attempt to stop using it failed.

Elizabeth was fighting her own addiction while trying to help Jackson with his. Bernadeta Bajda has been Elizabeth's housekeeper for many years. "I cried the entire time she asked for pills." She craved alcohol on occasion. We were advised not to give her alcohol, so we hid it high up where she couldn't find it. Jackson died on June 25, 2009, at his home in Holmby Hills, California. Conrad Murray, his personal doctor, was convicted of administering a deadly amount of anesthesia and propofol to him. When Elizabeth learned that Jackson had been admitted to the hospital, she instructed Mendelson to contact one of Jackson's assistants to find out how he was doing. "My Beloved Michael, I hope you remember how much I love you— and miss you," Elizabeth wrote Jackson in a letter that he would never read but that helped her grieve: "My Beloved Michael, I hope you remember how much I love you—and miss you." You are constantly on my mind and in my heart. My heart sounds like a high-pitched scream. I weep for you. I'm in a lot of pain. When am I going to see you again? I adore you and will always do so. Elizabeth, yours."

CHAPTER 17
Forgiveness

Carrie Fisher wrote a movie that was meant to be the female version of Grumpy Old Men. It turned into 2001's made-for-television movie These Old Broads, and Fisher cast Elizabeth and her mother in the film. The film's producer, Ilene Amy Berg, said that Elizabeth had bought an incredibly important piece of jewelry and told her that she wanted to buy earrings that matched it, and that she was doing the film so that she could buy the earrings. In her HBO standup show, Wishful Drinking, she joked: "My mother was Elizabeth's matron of honor. She even washed her hair on her wedding day. Now later I did hear her mumble that she wished she'd washed it with Nair, but she's not a bitter woman really." But the dark humor masked a real friendship she, and her mother, had struck with Elizabeth. In 2000, Fisher presented the GLAAD Vanguard award to her "stepmother Elizabeth Taylor" for her "bold support of the gay and lesbian community before the invention of the gay movement and her superhuman fight against AIDS."She said in a 2004 interview, "The best thing Elizabeth Taylor did for me was to get Eddie Fisher out of our house."

Debbie forgave Elizabeth, and both of them directed their rage towards Fisher, who treated them both poorly in the end. Fisher recounted intimate details about his connection with Elizabeth in his 1999 memoir: "Sexually, she was every man's dream; she had the face of an angel and the morals of a truck driver." Todd Fisher had overheard his mother on the phone with Elizabeth late at night several times in their lives. When he asked what they were discussing, she'd answer, "Just girl stuff." After all, they were some of the last people who remembered what it was like to be a celebrity in the 1950s. These Old Broads were shot on MGM's backlot. Elizabeth invited Debbie to her dressing room before filming an ironic scene in which Elizabeth's character steals Debbie's character's husband. Elizabeth recalled the past one last time, tears in her eyes. She attempted, piece by bit, to make amends with Debbie. Debbie had an incredible collection of movie memorabilia, and when she heard that one of Richard Burton's costumes from Cleopatra was being auctioned off for a price she couldn't afford, she called Elizabeth, who said she'd help her obtain it. Elizabeth was atoning for the perceived sin of ending an already-defunct marriage. It's unclear whether Elizabeth forgave Debbie for playing into the false story of the mistreated woman and contributing to Elizabeth's depiction as the villain.

"I've been lucky all my life," Elizabeth told Life magazine before turning sixty. I was given everything. Looks, fame, fortune, accolades, and love are all important. But I've paid for my good fortune with natural calamities, awful illnesses, devastating addictions, and shattered marriages." She felt much greater pain in 1997, when Princess Diana died in a vehicle accident after being pursued by paparazzi in a Paris tunnel. It reminded Elizabeth of all the near-death experiences she'd had. She retreated to her bed. He noticed she was suffering a seizure at that point and took her to the hospital. "They came into my room, all terribly doctor-like and solemn, and said, 'Elizabeth, you have a brain tumor.'" You've also suffered a seizure." It was less than a month before her 65th birthday, and she required surgery right away. She had already agreed to a televised black-tie event to raise funds for The Elizabeth Taylor AIDS Foundation in honor of her birthday. She was ecstatic about the organization she had founded, which focuses on direct patient care and has donated about $32 million since its founding. She felt she couldn't back out even though she was facing brain surgery because the event was raising money for AIDS, so she arranged the procedure for the day after the gala. She was back in her element after the procedure. She had spent so much time in hospitals, and she felt that this time she could make other individuals who were about to have brain surgery feel less fearful.

Throughout her life, Elizabeth exposed herself to the trauma of others. In the late 1990s, she went to the Lower East Side Needle Exchange (now known as the Lower East Side Harm Reduction Center) and met Dee, a woman in her thirties who had no teeth. Elizabeth was sensitive and compassionate, but she refused to let the physical and mental agony she witnessed destroy her. Even though she occasionally stayed in bed and did not always attend her own events, she still enjoyed hosting. For Sunday barbecues and holiday celebrations, forty or fifty people would show up. Clinton awarded her the Presidential Citizens Medal in 2001, the same year that famed boxer, activist, and poet Muhammad Ali received the award. "They made an immediate connection. "She was jokingly shushing them," recalled Michael Iskowitz, who escorted Clinton to the ceremony. The day was memorable, but it was also bittersweet for Elizabeth. Dr. Mathilde Krim, amfAR's cofounder, had earned the Presidential Medal of Freedom, a greater distinction, from Clinton the year before. Moshe Alon stated that Elizabeth harbored animosity for the slight. "She was concerned about receiving credit for her AIDS work." Elizabeth believed the Medal of Freedom belonged to her as well."

Elizabeth and Debbie Reynolds were in New York for concerts celebrating Michael Jackson's thirty-year solo career. On September 11, 2001, while they were there, the world changed forever. Elizabeth, like the rest of the country, was in mourning, and she felt powerless to help. Her chiropractor, Dr. Leroy Perry, was accompanying her on the trip. His niece worked in a building just behind the Twin Towers and had nowhere to stay because she lived in a block within the fallout zone. Elizabeth proposed that she join them at the St. Regis Hotel. Elizabeth presented her with shoes, clothes, a nice bath, and food. Elizabeth was unable to find a flight back to California, so she was forced to remain. She visited St. Patrick's Cathedral in New York and prayed for the victims of the assault. After that, Elizabeth wanted to help the police and firefighters at Ground Zero. She went to the armory near Ground Zero to console folks. Family and friends of the missing walked around with images of their loved ones and plastered them on the walls with banners asking if anyone had seen them.

Elizabeth had a desire to go to the World Trade Center site. Friends who were going with her were concerned about her health, but she pressed on, walking toward the disaster and joining a prayer circle along the route. It was 1:00 a.m. when Elizabeth returned from Ground Zero. She was pale, and she was having trouble breathing. She went to bed and slept for the majority of the next day. "I had to bring in oxygen to help her breath, and her blood pressure and pulse were elevated," said one of her doctors, LeRoy Perry, who was on the trip. Debbie Reynolds was staying at the Plaza Athénée, and Elizabeth urged her to stay at the St. Regis in a suite on the same floor so that they could be together. They flew out of town a few days later, but Elizabeth was very ill. Elizabeth was lonely near the end of her life and sometimes spent most of the day in her bedroom. According to Elizabeth Arden CEO Peter England, she called him at his house in Australia. She told her friends about how lonely she was. Her health was worsening when she was honored at the much-anticipated Kennedy Center Honors in Washington. When she got out of bed and stood up that morning, her blood pressure must have rapidly changed, leading her to collapse, she explained.

And she made it through her final performance onstage at Paramount Studios in Hollywood in 2007. She was 75 years old when she and James Earl Jones presented A. R. Gurney's play Love Letters to support The Elizabeth Taylor AIDS Foundation. She was in a wheelchair, but she looked stunning in a Michael Kors gown, a fur-trimmed cape, and Richard Burton's Van Cleef & Arpels diamond, coral, and amethyst earrings. She'd gone on stage for the first time in twenty-three years, and she was afraid. She had to negotiate a halt in a writer's strike in order to perform because she refused to cross the picket line. The strike had lasted almost a month, with picket lines built up at every studio on a daily basis. Patric Verrone, president of the Writers Guild at the time, recalled his assistant informing him of an urgent contact from Elizabeth Taylor.

Some facets of her personality were more pronounced as she grew older, such as her love of gifts and the game she made of receiving them. "Throughout her life, she developed the habit of attempting to elicit gifts from others. "I'm not sure what that was about, but she was pretty shameless about it at times, and being in her presence when she was trying to force someone to give her something was pretty embarrassing," Chris Wilding said. She requested a diamond tennis bracelet from Tom Cruise, but he wasn't sure what she wanted, so he sent her money instead. "I believe it was; do I still have it?" Can I still entice people? Joan Collins was one of the few persons who had the courage to say so. Elizabeth wanted to borrow a few of her bangle bracelets, but she refused. "She had a reputation for stealing people's jewelry." She didn't dwell on the past, but she did enjoy revisiting it from time to time. She always kept Richard dear to her heart; she loved it when the chandelier in her bedroom flickered because it meant Richard was on his way to see her.

CHAPTER 18
Dame Elizabeth

When Queen Elizabeth II appointed Elizabeth a dame, the female equivalent of a knight, in 2000, she refused to return the brooch that symbolized the accolade. Not even for a second. Before the investiture event, an advisor to the Queen assembled the group of awardees, which included Julie Andrews, at Buckingham Palace to brief them on what to anticipate. The Queen would affix the brooch, shake their hand, and they would curtsy and move to the cross hall. The brooch would be removed, placed in a box, and returned to them later. That was Elizabeth being herself, regardless of her surroundings. She appreciated gifts, and that brooch, a tribute to her years as an AIDS campaigner and humanitarian, was something she wanted to wear and admire right away. "Well, I've always been 'broad,'" she explained. "Now it's a great honor to be a dame!"

Elizabeth obtained approval later that day. She had, after all, traded wits and diamonds with Margaret and had been attended to by the Queen herself in 1976. Elizabeth sought clarification from her friend Sarah Ferguson, Duchess of York, who was briefly married to Prince Andrew, on the difference between the official titles "Lady" and "Dame." Dames are not permitted to use the title Lady unless they are married to a knight, a baron, or a life peer, the title of which cannot be inherited. Elizabeth had no idea she might have the honor because she lived in the United States, and she wanted to know what it signified.

Elizabeth was tired of being confined to her bedroom suite as she approached her seventies. She needed to get out of the home, so Tim Mendelson would drive her to the Abbey, a big homosexual club in West Hollywood, where she would sit in the rear wearing rhinestone sunglasses and knee-high boots, the more outrageous the attire, the better, and sip watermelon martinis surreptitiously. Ziv Ran, her security guard at the time, stated that she could see how her work as an activist had changed the reality for a generation of gay men. "I can't tell you how many gay men came up to her—dozens and dozens." Many people had tears in their eyes and went on bended knee to be eye level with her as she sat in her wheelchair. "You have no idea, but you saved my life," they stated. When Elizabeth informed the Abbey's creator, David Cooley, that it was her favorite bar, he had a plaque erected in her honor. Despite the fact that her later years were quieter, she had access to a rich emotional life as she drew on her memories. Every Yom Kippur, the Jewish community's holiest day of the year, she would call Ziv Ran into her bedroom and ask him to light a candle and read the Kiddush prayer for Mike Todd. Another extremely moving encounter occurred in 2010 at Buckingham Palace, when a bust of Richard Burton was revealed during a banquet commemorating the 60th anniversary of the Royal Welsh College of Music and Drama.

She was 78 years old and wheelchair-bound, and it had been three decades since she had divorced Richard for the last time, and more than twenty years since his death, but the striking bronze that was made for the foyer of a new theater named in his honor at Cardiff University in Wales overwhelmed her. When Elizabeth was seventy-four years old and partly in a wheelchair, she flew to Hawaii with Winters and his family and swam with sharks, but Mendelson remarked, "You couldn't talk her out of it." She adored animals, including sharks." "But isn't that the point?" She responded when she was ordered to remove her diamond jewelry because the light from the stones might attract too many sharks. She wore diamond bangles. She wanted to show people that she was having fun despite having terminal heart failure, osteoporosis, three hip replacements, and excruciating back pain.

Colin Farrell, who dated Britney Spears and is known for his rugged good features, was an unusual companion for Elizabeth, who was four decades his senior. They first met in 2009, when Tim Mendelson introduced himself to Farrell while Elizabeth was at Cedars-Sinai for a heart operation and Farrell was there for the birth of his son. After that, Farrell contacted his agent and requested her to schedule a meeting with Elizabeth; he couldn't stop thinking about her after he returned home from the hospital. He instructed his agent to send Elizabeth flowers, and she informed him that Elizabeth had already sent him orchids. "I thought that was freakin incredible. It's on! "I'm not sure who threw down the gauntlet, but it was thrown, and it shall be answered," he recalled with a chuckle. They finally met a few weeks later.

On a Saturday afternoon, he went to Nimes Road with a volume of poetry by William Butler Yeats that he had personalized to her. He waited in her back garden for an hour before she came downstairs. "She appeared to be lovely. Hair as tall as the Sears Tower, done up to perfection. She was stunning, beautiful, and full of life. Tim wheeled her out to me in a wheelchair. There was an unbelievable amount of dynamism to the conclusion." He leaned down next to her for a photograph as he was leaving, and he informed her that if she ever wanted him to come back and recite poetry to her, he would gladly oblige. He returned several times to read to her. He sat in an armchair by her bed, and she played recordings of Richard reading poems on occasion. His booming voice was blasted in via the room's speakers, and Farrell claimed it felt like Richard was present. She would close her eyes and imagine herself back in time with him. She grinned as she heard live audience applause over the speakers. They were both insomniacs, and occasionally he would call her house at two or three a.m., and her security guard would answer, and she would pick up thirty seconds later. "I was aware that I was a thirtysomething Dubliner on the phone with one of the most incredible human beings to walk the planet." They exchanged hundreds of texts during the course of their two-year acquaintance. Quinn, Elizabeth's grandson, was in his twenties at the time and recalls taunting Farrell and calling him "Papa Colin."

He was giving her something extraordinary in return, vitality at a time when she was feeling old and sick. Elizabeth loved how brash and tough and yet kind and romantic he was; it was the same with Richard, who could be tender and loving one minute and brooding and cruel the next. She wanted to see the younger version of herself in his eyes. Mendelson remembered watching Farrell take Elizabeth out on a dinner date to the Polo Lounge. "Moving Elizabeth had become a group effort at this point in her life. Just going out took a nurse, security, and me. But Colin picked her up, threw the wheelchair in the back of the car, and they sped off alone. It was really cool to see. Seeing them interact with each other was magical." Of course jewelry was a great love of her life, and Farrell gave her a diamond pendant necklace by Harry Winston. He knew that lavishing gifts upon her, just as Richard had done decades before, would make her smile, and that is what he wanted to do more than anything.

Society photographer Richard Young got his big break when he took a photograph of Elizabeth kissing Richard at his fiftieth birthday at the Dorchester Hotel in London in 1975. Elizabeth noticed him and told him in no uncertain terms to leave. But he sent her the photograph, and she loved it so much that she started inviting Young to events to photograph her. But he remembered seeing her the last time at an amfAR event at Cannes in a wheelchair and looking unwell. He refused to photograph her. People wanted to remember her as she was. Thirty years after Raintree County was released, Bob Dylan wrote Elizabeth a note from a hotel he was staying at in Chapel Hill, North Carolina. In it he captured how meaningful her life and her memories were to the story of Hollywood and the movie industry itself. To Dylan, and to so many of her fans, Elizabeth was captivating, not only because of what she personally accomplished as an actress, but also because of the legends who were her friends and who, at least in George Stevens's case, were occasionally her enemies. The last time the photographer Gianni Bozzacchi, who captured so much of Elizabeth and Richard's wild romance in the 1960s and early '70s, spoke with Elizabeth was a few weeks before she passed away. She had always loved his dirty jokes.

She maintained contact with John Warner and Ardeshir Zahedi during her time in Washington. Zahedi remembered their previous chat as well. "I spoke to her about ten days before she died while she was in the hospital." She replied she was exhausted, and I burst into tears." Nobody wanted to see her go through any more pain than she already had. When one of Elizabeth's nurses called him from the hospital to inform her kneecaps had cracked, Mendelson burst into tears. "I wept because I knew it was the end." She had advanced osteoporosis and was unable to walk or move due to damaged kneecaps. The agony was excruciating. He took her to the hospital on a weekly basis to get her lungs cleansed, but her body was eventually breaking down. Elizabeth was still prepared to travel to New York for a fundraiser for her favorite charity, amfAR, where she would be recognized alongside Bill Clinton and Diane von Furstenberg. But she never arrived. Her doctor told her the day she went to the hospital for the last time that the results of her blood work were so severe that she needed to be rushed to the emergency room right away. She left, but not before José Ever teased her hair to her liking and she did her own makeup, as she always did.

Colin Farrell and her children visited her in the intensive care unit. He wanted to get her home so she could die there. Mendelson concurred, but she stayed in the hospital. When they realized there was little hope of survival, Farrell said Mendelson, "Let's get a fucking ambulance and I'll just wheel her out." They won't be able to stop us." They could, however. Elizabeth remained in the hospital for six weeks before passing away from congestive heart failure on March 23, 2011, at the age of 79. She had so many beautiful loves, but she died alone. At her heart, she wished to be buried with Mike or Richard, but Sally Burton would not have approved of her being buried alongside Richard at Céligny. Elizabeth realized it was out of the question, so she fantasized about being buried in Wales, where she would have a link to him. While she talked about wanting to be buried with Mike, she couldn't get away from the horrible memory of what happened to his bones. She didn't want to be the victim of what had happened to him. When she went to Michael Jackson's memorial service at Forest Lawn Memorial Park in Glendale, she was stunned by its quiet beauty. Other celebrities, including her friends Spencer Tracy and Sammy Davis Jr., are buried among its beautiful three hundred acres. So she was eventually buried underneath a big white angel with outstretched arms.

Following Jewish tradition, a service was held immediately following her death with fifty members of her family and closest friends. Members of the Westboro Baptist Church threatened to disrupt the burial, and the daughter of the group's head took to Twitter to say, "No RIP Elizabeth Taylor who spent her life in adultery and enabling proud fags." Even after her death, Elizabeth seemed to irritate them. It would have been perfect for her. She was always herself—she stated in her will that any funeral or memorial event begin fifteen minutes late. Colin Farrell performed Elizabeth's favorite poem, "The Leaden Echo and the Golden Echo" by Victorian-era poet Gerard Manley Hopkins, at her funeral, surrounded by her closest friends and family. It's easy to see why Hopkins' poem, with its idea of giving up earthly beauty to God, meant so much to Elizabeth, who had always refused to be identified solely by her physical beauty. Following the funeral, a small group convened in Bungalow 5 at the Beverly Hills Hotel, which had formerly been Elizabeth's sanctuary and the place she went to escape the paparazzi.

Seven months after her death, a private memorial service was conducted on the Warner Brothers lot in Burbank. Farrell was the master of ceremonies, and before entering the service, he sat in his car in the parking lot, repeating what he was going to say. He wanted to get it right for Elizabeth since she meant so much to him. "It's easy for me to forget that we were friends," he admitted, "or to think of it as a fever dream." A performance of one of Elizabeth's favorite songs, "You'll Never Walk Alone" from the musical Carousel, was played, and Sir Elton John sang in front of 400 guests, including Michael Jackson's children, who paid tribute to Elizabeth's elegance and unwavering humanity. Elizabeth wished to be buried in all white, and she was, dressed in a white Badgley Mischka embroidered caftan and a white evening coat with a white fox collar, the same ensemble she had planned to wear to the amfAR event where she was to be honored shortly before she had to go to the hospital. She informed Mendelson that she did not want to be buried with any of her prized possessions.

CHAPTER 19
The Auction: "The Memory Always Brings Back a Stab of Joy, of Love"

Less than a year after her death, a record-breaking auction of her goods was held at Christie's in New York between December 13 and December 16, 2011. Elizabeth is thought to have owned the world's most costly private jewelry collection. The auction was so significant that Christie's employees who were thinking about retiring or changing careers waited until it was completed because they wanted the event on their resumes. The first night was the evening jewelry sale, which comprised an auction of eighty pieces of her most famous jewels. Christie's began the auction with home-video footage of Queen Elizabeth bidding on the Prince of Wales diamond brooch while sitting poolside in Bel Air. The atmosphere in the room was electrifying. The most treasured pieces were Richard and Mike's gifts, including the La Peregrina pearl, the Taj Mahal diamond, and the stunning ruby Cartier earrings, necklace, and bracelet that Mike Todd had given her poolside when she was pregnant with their daughter Liza. Buyers from thirty-six nations competed for the opportunity to possess a piece of Hollywood history. The 33.19-carat Krupp diamond, nicknamed the Elizabeth Taylor diamond, sold for $8.8 million, nearly three times its estimate, establishing a record price per carat for a colorless diamond. The sixteenth-century pear-shaped La Peregrina pearl sold for $11.8 million, above the expectation of $2 to $3 million. Mike Todd's tiara sold for $4.2 million, breaking the global record for a tiara.

That evening alone grossed about $116 million. The black-tie auction lasted more than eight hours as the auctioneers switched positions in a room packed with about 500 people. Her complete estate, including clothing, was worth more than $183 million at auction. At the time, it was the most costly jewelry sale in auction history. The majority of the products sold for more than ten times their greatest estimate. The low estimate for the entire sale was around $20 million, yet her jewelry alone brought around $144.2 million. In 2012, her paintings were auctioned individually at Christie's in London. Three of the most valued paintings sold for about $22 million, including a $16 million Van Gogh landscape. Daphne Lingon, a Christie's jewelry specialist, dubbed it "the most memorable auction of my career." Every day, thousands of people flocked to Christie's in New York to see the world-famous diamonds on display. The most wanted diamonds were the blingiest, but some of the less expensive but very personal objects, such as an ivory-and-gold necklace of eighteenth- and nineteenth-century engraved ivory opera passes that costume designer Edith Head left Elizabeth in her will, sold considerably beyond their estimate.

The necklace was expected to sell for between $1,500 and $2,000, but instead sold for $314,500. Elizabeth's mother acquired the antique costume pin for $25 ($380 in today's currencies) in the 1940s, and it was the first item of jewelry Elizabeth ever bought, sold for $74,500. It was expected to sell for $1,000 to $2,000. However, the pin came with a heartfelt thank you card from Elizabeth's mother. "The most extraordinary part of the sale was the room of jewelry boxes," André Leon Talley remarked. "The jewelry boxes alone were works of art." "Mike Todd Diamond Tiara," "Ping Pong Diamonds," and "Granny Necklace" (inside was a Van Cleef & Arpels gold-and-diamond choker with a diamond lion's face set with marquise-cut emerald eyes that Richard had bought her when she became a grandmother at thirty-eight years old). Everyone wanted a taste of Elizabeth's life as a princess or duchess from another country. She had everything produced by the world's top jewelers, including Boucheron, Bulgari, Van Cleef & Arpels, Jean Schlumberger, JAR, and Cartier. Her jewelry collection was one of the most flawless ever.

Stephen Lash, Christie's chairman, was impressed by Elizabeth's intelligence. "She brought to jewelry collecting the disciplines instilled in her by her father in art collecting." When you claim that collecting is difficult, you don't receive a lot of sympathy, yet collecting may be difficult if you want to do it correctly. And she did it exceptionally well." The basis for this historic auction was built decades before Elizabeth died. Lash began negotiations with Elizabeth's business consultants in the late 1970s that lasted for years, and they discussed her famed jewelry as well as her paintings, including a very valuable Frans Hals.

Curiel, then the head of Christie's jewelry department, traveled to Elizabeth's Bel Air house in 1998 to inspect her collection and evaluate its auction value. Christie's main rival, Sotheby's, also dispatched specialists to her residence. Curiel and two of his colleagues arrived at her house at 9:00 a.m. and sat at a large dining-room table covered in jewelry boxes. They began photographing and categorizing each item. "I didn't dare to ask if she would come, but we heard some noise on the second floor of the house from time to time," he explained. "At eleven o'clock, Elizabeth Taylor came down the staircase in a caftan. She sat with us and spent the rest of the day scrutinizing every item of jewelry. And what impressed me the most was how well she knew each piece. We were staring at a sapphire when she stated, "This sapphire looks like a Kashmir sapphire, but it's not a Kashmir, it's a Burma stone."

The inclusion indicates that it is Burmese. It was marketed to me as Kashmir, and I'm not pleased.' I was enthralled. It was as if I were speaking with a professional. The entire day was like this; she knew every jewel by heart, who gave it to her, and who gave it to her. Eddie Fisher, she claimed, didn't know anything about jewelry. 'He thought he was giving me a wonderful gift, but look at the quality of the stone,' she commented as they studied a piece. 'It appears to be large, but it is of poor quality, and the poor man was unaware. 'I'm sure he got taken advantage of.'" Curiel was shocked since she knew the geographical origin of the stone, the quality of the stone, and the way it was carved. "I spent a day there with someone who knew everything there was to know about stones and with whom I could have very interesting discussions." Typically, this is attributed to Van Cleef & Arpels or Cartier. They don't truly understand their stones. It seemed like I was sitting with a jeweler." Every jewel that Mike Todd or another husband had given her had a small tag with her handwriting on the box. The jewelry boxes labeled "Richard Burton" and "Mike Todd" had an effect on her, bringing back memories. They were never far from the surface to begin with. She told Curiel when she received each item and what it meant to her. It occurred to him that this might be the first time that every single piece has been placed out on a table together.

Christie's went all-in to win the contract to be her auction house. Nancy Valentino, a Christie's employee who had assisted in the then-record-breaking sale of "The Personal Property of Marilyn Monroe" in 1999, went to Elizabeth's chalet in Gstaad to take inventory in 2000. "She hadn't been there in seven years, and it was as if someone had made toast in her kitchen that day." The hairbrush included hair. It was as though [the Burtons] had never left!" Chalet Ariel symbolized her life with Richard, a life filled with marriage and children. Valentino was accompanied by Chris Wilding, Liza Todd Tivey, and Tim Mendelson as they looked through the house selecting what should be retained and sent to Bel Air and what should be sold. Elizabeth was familiar with every piece of furniture in the house. They only had five days to clear out the entire house, which had already been sold, and determine what was valuable enough to include in the auction. It was upsetting for Elizabeth's children, who had seen Gstaad as a haven from the outside world and their mother's enormous celebrity and turbulent personal life. It was their only home; the rest of the time, their mother lived on a yacht, in opulent hotels, and in short-term residences.

Valentino cataloged over three thousand pieces of jewelry in a separate room. The property was crammed with Elizabeth and Richard's belongings, including 72 1960s wigs stashed in one of the closets. Christie's worked hard to gain Elizabeth's trust, including throwing a gala at Christie's in Rockefeller Center to commemorate the publication of her 2002 book, My Love Affair with Jewelry. They realized her jewelry told the tale of her life. Some of her jewelry was meant to go on display in Europe to commemorate the publication of the book, but she couldn't let them leave, so they were returned to Los Angeles. She compared each piece to one of her children. She'd let them free eventually, but only once she was gone. They were too important to her.

Jennifer Tilly, a big jewelry collector, recalled the auction's enthusiasm. "I'd always wanted a piece of Cleopatra jewelry because I'd read about her hanging out on the Via Veneto in Rome and going into the Bulgari store, where they'd open vats of jewels." I wanted something from that era because she was in love with Richard Burton at the time." But, she added, the auction prices were becoming too high, and with Bulgari buying back some of its pieces, she ended up purchasing a yellow-and-white diamond brooch from Eddie Fisher. "When they divorced, she paid off the brooch bill, which was incredible because she never paid for her own jewelry." So I assumed she must have adored this brooch!"

Elizabeth would have been pleased to hear that her jewelry was valued by its new owners. The diamonds were on a three-month global tour that included stops in Moscow, London, Los Angeles, Dubai, Geneva, Paris, Hong Kong, and New York, with record audiences in each location. Elizabeth's jewelry was always about her travels and the people she cared about. Because she didn't keep her jewelry in a vault and preserve it for special events, but wore it every day, it became a part of her, and everyone desired a piece even after she died. Valentino cataloged over three thousand pieces of jewelry in a separate room. The property was crammed with Elizabeth and Richard's belongings, including 72 1960s wigs stashed in one of the closets. Christie's worked hard to gain Elizabeth's trust, including throwing a gala at Christie's in Rockefeller Center to commemorate the publication of her 2002 book, My Love Affair with Jewelry. They realized her jewelry told the tale of her life. Some of her jewelry was meant to go on display in Europe to commemorate the publication of the book, but she couldn't let them leave, so they were returned to Los Angeles. She compared each piece to one of her children. She'd let them free eventually, but only once she was gone. They were too important to her.

Jennifer Tilly, a big jewelry collector, recalled the auction's enthusiasm. "I'd always wanted a piece of Cleopatra jewelry because I'd read about her hanging out on the Via Veneto in Rome and going into the Bulgari store, where they'd open vats of jewels." I wanted something from that era because she was in love with Richard Burton at the time." But, she added, the auction prices were becoming too high, and with Bulgari buying back some of its pieces, she ended up purchasing a yellow-and-white diamond brooch from Eddie Fisher. "When they divorced, she paid off the brooch bill, which was incredible because she never paid for her own jewelry." So I assumed she must have adored this brooch!"

Elizabeth would have been pleased to hear that her jewelry was valued by its new owners. The diamonds were on a three-month global tour that included stops in Moscow, London, Los Angeles, Dubai, Geneva, Paris, Hong Kong, and New York, with record audiences in each location. Elizabeth's jewelry was always about her travels and the people she cared about. Because she didn't keep her jewelry in a vault and preserve it for special events, but wore it every day, it became a part of her, and everyone desired a piece even after she died.

Made in United States
Troutdale, OR
11/29/2023

15104001R00080